Moon River and Magnolias

A Collection of Southern Recipes for Family and Friends

Debra Arrington and Dorothy Arrington
Savannah, Georgia

Copyright © 2016
Morris Press Cookbooks
All rights reserved. Reproduction in whole or
in part without written permission is prohibited.

Printed in the USA by

800-445-6621 • www.morriscookbooks.com
P.O. Box 2110 • Kearney, NE 68848

Dedication

It is only fitting that this book be dedicated to the one person who gave us the encouragement it took for us to take on such a project, my Dad.

He was our reason for creating and cooking hundreds of dishes for the many years we were together as a family. It was his love for us and the appreciation he had for what we prepared that made every meal a fond memory.

We miss all of those warm, happy times we had together but most of all we miss the one that made our family complete, my wonderful Dad.

*"Warm summer sun, Shine kindly here,
Warm southern wind, Blow softly here..."*

Mark Twain

Warm Southern Memories

The soft warm breezes of a summer's evening when the heat of the day had broken is one of my fondest memories when growing up in the South. It was a happy time because busy cares of the day were ending and soon the family would be coming together around the supper table. The kitchen was the heart of our home, the coziest, happiest room in the house because that's where you found us gathered while Mama was putting the finishing touches on one of her delicious meals. I remember how the aroma of fried chicken would fill the kitchen while a pot of peppered greens simmered on the stove. In the oven was a pan of flaky buttermilk biscuits baking and cooling on the kitchen table was a fresh peach pie.

Mama was always busy in the kitchen. I never remember her having an idle moment. Much love and care went into each and every delicious meal we had whether it was a simple summer lunch or a feast for a family reunion.

Good food has always been an important part of our Southern heritage. In our family as in many Southern families there were generations of good cooks. My Great-Grandmother had a remarkable reputation all of her life for her Southern cooking and her talent passed on to my Grandmother, my Mother and according to family and friends, to myself.

The recipes you'll find tucked in the pages of this book are favorites of our family. Some are more recent creations suited for the hectic lives we all live now while others date back generations.

You'll find delightful breakfast, brunch and lunch dishes that you'll enjoy preparing for family, friends and weekend guests.

There's a large variety of soups, salads, sides and main dishes to choose from that will give your meals a true Southern flair and let you show your "Southern hospitality" to your friends no matter where you live.

The most important part of a Southerner's lunch or dinner is dessert. In fact, when talking on the phone with dear friends that are separated from us by thousands of miles the last thing they ask is "What's for dessert?"! The south is known for its wide variety of sweet confections so to top off your lunches or suppers we've included some old Southern favorites.

Our family were "nightowls" and although we always had a big supper and dessert each evening we would enjoy munching late at night after playing games or watching a late movie. We've added many snacks for you to have with your "nightowls" or to enjoy at your next patio party.

Our recipes are full of many delicious ingredients but the most important ingredient to have when preparing any meal for your family and friends is LOVE. With that one ingredient the simplest meal can be a feast. My Mother and I still enjoy cooking together for ourselves but one of the biggest joys in life comes from preparing meals to share with friends so dear to our heart.

We have enjoyed writing this book and hope that these cherished family recipes will become favorites for your family to enjoy now and for years to come.

We're looking forward to sharing even more with you in the future. Till then...

                        Bon Appétit, Y'all
                        Debra and Dorothy Arrington

Table of Contents

Breakfast, Brunch And Lunch 1

Appetizers And Sandwiches 15

Soups And Salads 29

Vegetables And Sides 53

Main Dishes 71

Breads And Biscuits 91

Desserts And Beverages 95

Relishes, Butters And Sauces 107

Index 115

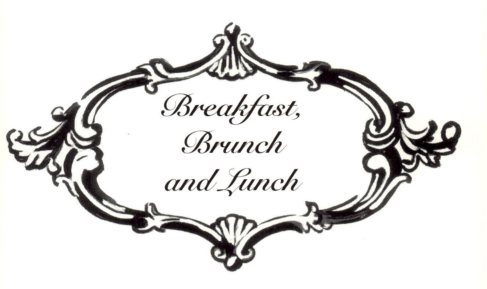

Helpful Hints

- Unbaked cookie dough can be covered and refrigerated for up to 24 hours or frozen in an airtight container for up to 9 months.

- Bake one cookie sheet at a time on the middle oven rack.

- Decorate cookies with chocolate by placing cookies on a rack over waxed paper. Dip the tines of a fork into melted chocolate and wave the fork gently back and forth to make line decorations.

- Some cookies need indentations on top to fill with jam or chocolate. Use the rounded end of a honey dipper.

- Dip cookie cutters in flour or powdered sugar and shake off excess before cutting. For chocolate dough, dip cutters in baking cocoa.

- Tin coffee cans make excellent freezer containers for cookies.

- If you only have one cookie sheet on hand, line it with parchment paper. While one batch is baking, load a second sheet of parchment paper to have another batch ready to bake. Cleanup will be easier.

- When a recipe calls for packed brown sugar, fill the correct size measuring cup with sugar and use one cup size smaller to pack the brown sugar into its cup.

- Cut-up dried fruit often sticks to the blade of your knife. To prevent this problem, coat the blade of your knife with a thin film of vegetable spray before cutting.

- Instead of folding nuts into brownie batter, sprinkle on top of batter before baking. This keeps nuts crunchy instead of soggy.

- Only use glass or shiny metal pans. Dark or nonstick pans will cause brownies to become soggy and low in volume.

- When making bars, line pan with aluminum foil and prepare as directed. The bars can be lifted out, and cleanup is easy.

- Cutting bars is easier if you score the bars right as the pan leaves the oven. When the bars cool, cut along the scored lines.

- Use a double boiler for melting chocolate to prevent it from scorching. A slow cooker on the lowest setting also works well for melting chocolate, especially when coating a large amount of candy.

- Parchment paper provides an excellent nonstick surface for candy. Waxed paper should not be used for high-temperature candy.

Breakfast, Brunch And Lunch

FARM-STYLE APPLE WALNUT FRENCH TOAST

8 slices cinnamon-raisin bread
2 T. butter
2 med. Granny Smith apples, peeled and cut in thin wedges
½ c. chopped walnuts
1½ T. light brown sugar

2 eggs, beaten
⅓ c. half-and-half
⅛ tsp. salt
½ tsp. vanilla
Oil

Slice bread slices diagonally and set aside. In small skillet, melt butter. Add apples and walnuts and sauté 5 minutes. Sprinkle with brown sugar and continue tossing until apples are firm soft and glazed. Set aside and keep warm. In shallow pan, combine beaten egg, half-and-half, salt and vanilla. Heat oil in large skillet. Dip bread in egg mixture and fry until golden. Keep warm until all slices have been fried. Serve toast by topping with apple walnut mixture.

Note: Crispy fried bacon pairs off with this country morning breakfast favorite. Be sure to serve with whipped butter and warm maple syrup.

River Street Beer Battered French Toast with Cheese Sauce

3 lg. eggs
⅓ c. beer
½ c. half-and-half
½ tsp. salt
½ tsp. garlic powder
1 (15-oz.) jar cheese spread
1 (2-oz.) jar pimiento, drained
Oil for frying

In mixing bowl, whisk eggs until frothy. Whisk in beer, half-and-half, salt and garlic powder. Set aside. In small saucepan, heat cheese spread until soft. Add pimiento and continue heating until bubbly. Reduce heat and keep warm (adding a few drops of milk, if needed, for thinning). In large skillet, heat oil. Dip bread in egg-beer mixture and fry until golden and puffed, turning as needed. Serve topped with cheese sauce.

Note: Dish this up with some red hot sausage links and you'll feel like you're in the heart of the "Big Easy!"

Spicy Savory French Toast with Cheesy Crab Sauce

12 (½-inch thick) slices day-old French bread
3 eggs, beaten
¼ c. heavy cream
1 lg. clove garlic, crushed
2 tsp. hot sauce
½ tsp. salt
1½ c. crushed cornflakes
Oil for frying
2 c. Cheesy Crab Sauce

Slice and set aside French bread. In mixing bowl, combine eggs, cream, garlic, hot sauce and salt. Set aside. In shallow pan, crush cornflakes until finely crumbled. Heat oil in skillet. Dip bread slices in egg mixture and heavily dredge in cornflake crumbs. Fry 2 to 3 slices of bread at a time until golden brown on both sides. Keep warm in 250° oven until all pieces have been fried. Serve with Cheesy Crab Sauce.

Cheesy Crab Sauce:

1 (16-oz.) jar cheddar cheese sauce
½ c. cooked, flaked crab meat
2 T. finely chopped pimiento
½ tsp. Creole seasoning

In medium saucepan, combine cheese sauce, crab, pimiento and seasoning. Blend well and heat over medium heat until hot and bubbly. Keep warm until serving.

Note: This New Orleans inspired brunch dish will make you think you're dining under the moss draped trees in the French Quarter Courtyards.

Quick 'N Easy Ham 'N Biscuit Bake

1 c. biscuit mix
2 c. cubed, cooked smoked ham
1 (15-oz.) can baby green lima beans
½ c. pickled pearl onions
2 c. white sauce
½ tsp. black pepper
½ tsp. cayenne

Prepare biscuit mix according to package directions and set aside. In large mixing bowl, combine ham, lima beans, onions, white sauce, black pepper and cayenne pepper. Toss to blend well. Turn into 2-quart casserole. Drop biscuit dough by teaspoon over top of casserole. Bake in preheated 375° oven for 30 minutes or until bubbly and biscuit topping is golden brown.

Note: Just got a call and found out company is coming? This is ready in less than an hour and looks like you worked all day on it. Serve with a platter of sliced fresh tomatoes, corn on the cob and sweet butter.

Southern Ham 'N Biscuits with Country Pepper Gravy

2 c. flour
3 T. baking powder
½ tsp. salt
½ tsp. onion powder
½ c. shortening
⅔ c. buttermilk
½ c. finely chopped ham
Pepper gravy

Combine flour, baking powder, salt and onion powder. Cut in shortening until resembles coarse crumbs. Make a well and add buttermilk and ham. Stir quickly with fork until soft dough forms. Turn onto lightly floured surface. Knead 10 to 12 strokes. Pat out to ½ inch thick and cut 2-inch biscuits. Bake at 450° for 12 to 15 minutes. Serve with Pepper Gravy.

Pepper Gravy:

4 T. butter
4 T. flour
½ tsp. salt
1½ tsp. black pepper
¼ tsp. ground red pepper
2 c. milk

In saucepan, melt butter over low heat. Blend flour, salt and peppers. Add milk all at once whisking until smooth. Cook quickly, stirring constantly until mixture thickens and bubbles. Remove from heat and serve with biscuits.

Note: This is such an easy brunch entree to serve. There's not a lot of preparation. The ham is in the biscuits.

CREAMED HAM OVER ONION CHEESE BISCUITS

Onion Cheese Biscuits:

2 c. flour
3 T. baking powder
½ tsp. salt
½ c. shortening

⅔ c. buttermilk
½ c. grated cheddar cheese
2 T. finely minced onion

Combine flour, baking powder and salt; cut in shortening until mixture resembles coarse crumbs. Make a well and add buttermilk, cheese and minced onions. stir with fork until soft dough forms. Turn onto lightly floured surface. Knead 10 to 12 strokes. Pat out to ½ inch thick and cut 2-inch biscuits. Bake in preheated 450° oven for 12 to 15 minutes or until golden. While biscuits are baking, prepare Creamed Ham.

Creamed Ham:

2 T. butter
4 T. flour
½ tsp. salt

2 c. milk
1½ c. fine, cubed ham

In medium skillet, melt butter. Whisk in flour and salt along with milk until smooth and free of lumps. Add ham and continue cooking over medium heat stirring constantly. When thickened, reduce heat and keep warm until biscuits come out of oven. While biscuits are hot, split in half and place on individual luncheon plates. Ladle Creamed Ham over biscuits. Serve hot.

Note: For a dainty ladies luncheon, try serving with chilled tomato juice cocktail, deviled eggs and watermelon preserves.

CORNY CHICKEN SQUARES

⅓ c. chopped celery
¼ c. chopped bell pepper
⅓ c. chopped green onion
2 (6½-oz.) pkgs. corn muffin mix
2 eggs
1 c. chicken broth

2 c. finely chopped, cooked chicken
2 T. oil
½ tsp. ground sage
½ tsp. salt
¾ tsp. ground red pepper

Sauté celery and bell pepper in small skillet until tender. Add green onion and sauté 5 minutes longer. In mixing bowl, combine muffin mix, eggs and chicken broth. Mix until blended. Add celery mixture, chicken, oil, sage, salt and ground red pepper. Pour mixture into greased 13 x 9-inch baking pan and bake 30 minutes at 400° or until tests done.

Note: An easy recipe for a mid-day brunch with the girls. Let your imagination take over and top with one of your favorite sauces.

SUNRISE BREAKFAST CASSEROLE

1 (16-oz.) pkg. frozen potatoes O'Brien, prepared according to pkg. directions
6 lg. eggs
2 oz. cream cheese, softened

12 breakfast sausage links, pan fried
1 c. shredded Colby-Jack cheese
¼ c. chopped chives

Butter a 2-quart casserole. Line bottom with prepared potatoes. Set aside. In skillet, whisk eggs and cream cheese together. Softly scramble over low heat until slightly under done (will finish cooking in final step of recipe). Split cooked sausage links lengthwise. Spoon egg mixture over potatoes and arrange sausage links in geometric pattern on top of eggs. Sprinkle with shredded cheese and top with chives. Place in oven at 375° for 10 to 15 minutes or until cheese is melted and bubbly.

Note: For weekend guests, nothing is simpler or more attractive for your breakfast or brunch table. It's perfectly complete when accompanied by a pot of hot coffee, oven toast and a fresh fruit bowl.

MOLLY'S MAC 'N CHICKEN CASSEROLE

4 c. cooked elbow macaroni
1 c. shredded cheddar cheese
½ tsp. onion powder
¼ c. chopped pimiento
1 (10¾-oz.) can cream of chicken soup

½ c. milk
⅓ c. cracker crumbs
2 T. butter

In large mixing bowl, combine macaroni with cheese, onion powder and pimiento. Toss well. In separate bowl, blend chicken soup with milk until thoroughly smooth. Pour over macaroni mixture and toss until well blended. Place mixture in large baking dish. Sprinkle with cracker crumbs and dot with butter. Bake at 375° for 30 minutes or until golden brown.

Note: Whether you're going on a picnic, a day on the river or if it's your turn to have the garden club members on your patio, this is the perfect answer. Serve with a crisp green salad, hard rolls and butter and, of course, Southern Sweet Tea.

THIN CRISP LEMON PANCAKES WITH SALMON DILL CHEESE

1 c. pancake mix, prepared according to directions on box for thin pancakes
2 tsp. grated lemon peel
½ c. broiled, flaked salmon
½ c. ricotta cheese
1 tsp. dill weed
1 tsp. lemon juice
½ tsp. garlic powder
½ tsp. salt
Hollandaise Sauce
Thin sliced lemon

To pancake batter, add lemon peel, blend and set aside. In small mixing bowl, combine salmon, cheese, dill, lemon juice, garlic powder and salt. Blend well. Set aside. On hot greased griddle, cook pancakes. Divide filling between pancakes and spoon down center of each pancake. Loosely roll and place seam side down in lightly buttered casserole dish.

Hollandaise Sauce:

⅔ c. sour cream
⅓ c. mayonnaise
2 T. fresh lemon juice
2 tsp. yellow mustard
½ tsp. salt

In small saucepan, whisk together sour cream, mayonnaise, lemon juice, mustard and salt. Heat over medium heat stirring constantly. Thin with a little milk, if necessary. Keep warm until serving. Cover casserole tightly with foil and heat in 350° oven for 15 minutes or until hot. Remove from oven. Serve on individual plates or platter and drizzle with Hollandaise Sauce. Garnish with thin lemon slices.

Note: Although this is a very elegant dish it's so easy to prepare. The hollandaise is so simple and it is eggless!

SPICY FISH POCKETS

6 (3-inch) pieces of white fish fillets
½ tsp. ground red pepper
Salt to taste
½ tsp. garlic powder
1 T. butter, cut into 6 pieces

1 (17-oz.) pkg. puff pastry (2 sheets)
⅓ c. salsa
6 slices Pepper-Jack cheese
1 egg, beaten

Season fish fillet pieces with red pepper, salt and garlic powder. Place on broiler pan and top each fillet piece with butter. Broil for 15 minutes or until fish flakes easily. Remove from oven and let cool. Roll puff pastry sheets on lightly floured surface to ⅛ inch thick. Cut 6 (6-inch) rounds. Place 1 fillet on each pastry round. Divide salsa between rounds and top each fillet. Place slice of cheese over salsa. Brush ½-inch border of circles with beaten egg. Fold over and crimp with fork to seal. Place on parchment-lined baking pan and brush with remaining beaten egg. Bake in preheated 375° oven for 25 to 35 minutes or until puffed and golden brown.

Note: Delicious when served with a cup of Mama's Shrimp Bisque!

SEASIDE MAC 'N CHEESE

2 T. butter
3 T. flour
¼ tsp. salt
1½ c. milk
⅓ c. heavy cream
¼ tsp. cayenne pepper
½ tsp. minced garlic

4 c. cooked elbow macaroni
1 c. salad shrimp
½ c. flaked crab meat
1 c. shredded cheddar cheese
1 c. shredded Muenster cheese
½ c. cracker crumbs
2 T. butter

In saucepan over low heat, melt butter. Stir in flour and salt. Add milk and cream all at once. Stirring constantly, add cayenne pepper and garlic. Continue cooking until mixture thickens. Remove from heat and set aside. In large bowl, combine cooked macaroni, shrimp and crab. Fold in cream mixture and cheeses until blended. Turn into buttered casserole. Top with crumbs and dot with butter. Bake in 375° oven for 35 minutes until golden and bubbly.

Note: A great make-ahead dish for a day on the boat. Pair it with a tossed green salad for a delicious lunch or brunch.

DAD'S SUNDAY MORNIN' EGGS

8 eggs
4 T. heavy cream
½ tsp. dill weed
½ tsp. garlic powder
⅓ c. cottage cheese
Salt and pepper according to taste

In large mixing bowl, whisk eggs until lemon color. Add cream, dill weed, garlic powder, cottage cheese and salt and pepper. Cook eggs in heavy skillet over medium heat stirring occasionally with spoon so that large soft curds form. Do not overcook.

Note: Many a Sunday morning Mama and I woke up to the aroma of oven toast, coffee and Dad's specialty, his "Sunday Mornin' Eggs." It was such a warm, fuzzy feeling to wake up and hear him pattering in the kitchen while we were still snug in our beds.

BEAUFORT BREAKFAST SANDWICH

6 slices thick-sliced bologna
2 T. oil
6 lg. eggs
6 extra lg. buttermilk biscuits hot from the oven

Make 5 (½-inch) cuts around edges of bologna slices (this prevents them from curling when fried). In hot greased skillet, pan fry slices until lightly browned and crisp around the edges. Set aside and keep warm. In small skillet, add oil and hard fry eggs until yolks are semi-soft but not runny. Split hot biscuits and sandwich slice of bologna and egg in each biscuits. Serve immediately or wrap in foil and keep warm in oven until serving time.

Note: This recipe is from a Beaufort, South Carolina boarding house where my family was staying during the war in the summer of 1944.

Corn Fried Tomatoes with Pimiento Cheese Sauce

3 lg. green tomatoes, sliced ¼ inch thick
½ c. flour
1 c. pancake mix
1 c. water
1 ¾ c. fine corn flake crumbs
½ tsp. salt
½ tsp. paprika
½ tsp. garlic powder
½ tsp. black pepper
Oil for frying

In shallow pan, dredge tomatoes in flour and set aside. In small mixing bowl, whisk together pancake mix and water. Set aside. In medium pan, blend together corn flake crumbs, salt, paprika, garlic powder and black pepper. Dip flour coated tomato slices in pancake batter then heavily dredge in corn flake crumbs. Fry in hot oil until golden and crisp. Serve with cheese sauce.

Pimiento Cheese Sauce:

2 T. flour
½ c. sour cream
¾ c. milk
¼ tsp. salt
1 c. grated cheddar cheese
2 T. chopped pimiento

Whisk flour and sour cream into milk in 1½-quart saucepan. Add salt. Cook over medium heat until sauce begins to thicken. Add cheese and pimiento and continue to cook over medium heat until cheese is melted.

Note: These fried green tomatoes, a favorite in the South, make a fantastic appetizer, are great as a main dish for lunch when accompanied with crispy fried bacon or tops off any summer evening supper on the porch.

Spring Garden Quiche

1 (9-inch) unbaked pie shell
1½ c. grated cheddar cheese
½ c. canned asparagus tips, drained
3 eggs
¾ c. heavy cream
¾ c. milk
½ tsp. salt
½ tsp. black pepper
1 tsp. dried parsley
6 thin slices tomato, patted dry
3 sprigs fresh dill

Place unbaked pie pastry in 400° oven and bake 5 minutes. Remove from oven and let cool. When cool, sprinkle cheddar cheese over crust and top with asparagus tips. Set aside. In mixing bowl, whisk eggs, cream, milk, salt, pepper and parsley together. Pour over cheese and asparagus. Return to oven and bake at 375° for 35 minutes. Remove from oven and arrange tomato slices and dill sprigs on top. Return to oven and continue baking 10 to 15 minutes longer or until lightly browned on top.

Note: Quiches are a great way to entertain. They give you, the hostess, more time with your guests. Quiche can be made a day or two in advance. After cooling, refrigerate in an airtight container. Before serving, heat in 350° oven for 10 to 15 minutes or until warm.

Harvest-Time Golden Corn Quiche

1 (9-inch) pie shell
4 slices bacon, cooked crisp and crumbled
⅓ c. chopped red bell pepper
⅓ c. chopped onion
⅔ c. cream-style corn
¾ c. half-and-half
4 eggs, slightly beaten
¼ tsp. salt
½ tsp. black pepper
1 c. grated cheddar cheese

In 450° oven, bake pie shell 5 to 7 minutes. Remove and set aside. In skillet, fry bacon until crisp, remove and sauté bell pepper and onion in 2 tablespoons of bacon fat. Set aside. In mixing bowl, combine corn, half-and-half and eggs. Blend well; stir in salt and pepper. Crumble bacon and sprinkle over bottom of pie shell. Follow with bell pepper and onion. Sprinkle grated cheese over all. Pour corn mixture into shell. Bake in preheated 375° oven for 35 to 40 minutes or until tests done.

Note: Perfect for a garden club luncheon! Add a tossed salad and a cup of soup and you're all set!

DEEP SOUTH HAM AND APPLE QUICHE

1 (9-inch) frozen pie shell, thawed
¾ c. diced ham
½ c. diced apple
½ c. diced onion
¾ c. shredded Colby-Jack cheese
2 lg. eggs
2 egg yolks
¾ c. milk
¾ c. cream
Salt and pepper to taste

Partially bake pie shell according to package directions. Set aside. In skillet, sauté ham, apple and onion until onion is transparent. Remove from heat. Spread ham mixture and cheese evenly over bottom of pie shell. In medium bowl, whisk egg, egg yolks, milk and cream until blended. Add salt and pepper to taste. Pour egg mixture to ¼ inch below crust rim (you may have extra; don't over fill). Bake 35 minutes in preheated 375° oven until lightly golden brown and knife blade inserted near the edge comes out clean and center feels set but soft. Serve warm or at room temperature.

Note: A wonderful way to start the morning with house guests. You can prepare it the day before and heat is up in the morning. Serve with home fried potatoes and a fresh fruit cup.

LOW COUNTRY CHICKEN LIVERS

1 lb. chicken livers, rinsed and drained
1 c. all-purpose flour
Oil
1 bell pepper, chopped
1 lg. onion, chopped
3 T. all-purpose flour
1 c. chicken broth
¾ c. diced canned tomatoes, drained
Salt and pepper to taste
¼ tsp. ground red pepper

Dredge livers in flour. Heat oil in skillet. Fry livers in small batches until golden brown. Remove from oil and drain on paper towels. Discard oil reserving 4 tablespoons in skillet. Add bell pepper and sauté 5 minutes. Then add onion and sauté until golden. Remove from skillet and set aside. In remaining oil in skillet, add 3 tablespoons flour and cook over medium heat to a dark golden roux. Gradually add broth whisking all the while to prevent lumps. When smooth, return pepper and onion mixture to skillet along with tomatoes. Season with salt and pepper and ground red pepper. Simmer 5 to 7 minutes.

Note: Serve over hot, fluffy rice and pass the gravy!

LADIES' LUNCHEON PIMIENTO CHEESE PIE

1 (16-oz.) ctn. cottage cheese
3 eggs, slightly beaten
1 T. mayonnaise
1½ c. shredded cheddar cheese
¼ c. chopped pimiento
¼ tsp. salt
1 (9-inch) pie shell

In mixing bowl, blend cottage cheese and eggs. Stir in mayonnaise. Fold in cheddar cheese, pimiento and salt. When well blended, turn into pie shell and bake in 375° preheated oven for 40 minutes or until knife inserted in center comes out clean.

Note: When served with a crisp apple salad and steaming cup of soup, this cheese pie makes a most elegant brunch for the girls. It can be made a day ahead and reheated 350° for 10 to 15 minutes or until warm.

RICE PLANTERS BRUNCH

½ lb. ground hot sausage
1 sm. onion, chopped
¼ c. chopped pecans
1 c. sliced white mushrooms
¼ c. sliced water chestnuts, drained
2 c. cooked long-grain and wild rice
1 (14½-oz.) can cream of mushroom soup
8 eggs
4 T. butter

In skillet, sauté sausage for 5 minutes. Add onions and pecans and sauté 5 minutes more. Add mushrooms and water chestnuts. Continue sautéing until mushrooms are soft. Combine with cooked rice and fold in cream of mushroom soup. Divide mixture between 4 greased ramekins. Make well in center of each serving. Place 2 eggs in each well; dot with butter. Bake in preheated 350° oven until eggs are set.

Note: Rice plantations are a part of our Southern heritage and many of our dishes are based around rice. This is a true plantation brunch when served with sour cream and chive biscuits, ice cold tomato juice and sweet tea.

SAVORY CRAB CHEESECAKE

¾ c. cracker crumbs
4 T. melted butter
¼ tsp. garlic powder
¼ tsp. black pepper
1 T. butter
¼ c. chopped bell pepper
1½ tsp. minced garlic

3 eggs
2 (8-oz.) pkgs. cream cheese
¼ tsp. salt
1 T. flour
½ tsp. prepared mustard
2 c. sour cream
¾ c. lump crabmeat

In medium mixing bowl, blend crumbs, melted butter, garlic powder and black pepper until mixed. Press in bottom and up ⅔ of sides of 8-inch springform pan. Chill while preparing filling. **Filling:** In small pan, sauté in butter the bell pepper until softened. Add garlic and sauté 1 to 2 minutes longer. Remove from heat and let cool. In large mixing bowl, beat until smooth the eggs and cream cheese. Add salt, flour and mustard. Stir in sour cream. Fold in crab and pepper mixture. Pour into prepared crust and bake at 375° for 35 to 45 minutes or until knife inserted off center comes out clean.

Note: When making this in an 8-inch springform pan, cut into wedges for an elegant brunch. Serve with a steaming cup of cream of tomato soup and Caesar salad. Or make it into mini tartlets for hors d'oeuvre at your next special occasion.

LOW COUNTRY SPOON BREAD

8 T. melted margarine
1 (8-oz.) can cream-style corn
1 (8-oz.) can whole kernel corn, drained
1 c. sour cream
2 eggs, beaten

1 (7-oz.) pkg. corn muffin mix
½ c. flaked crab meat
¼ c. chopped onion, sautéed
¼ c. chopped bell pepper, sautéed
⅛ c. chopped celery, sautéed

Heat oven to 375°. Grease 1½-quart casserole dish. In a greased casserole, add margarine and corn. Blend in sour cream. Add eggs and stir well. Blend in corn muffin mix. Blend thoroughly. Fold in crab, onion, pepper and celery. Bake 35 to 45 minutes or until tests done.

Note: This has been a favorite of family and friends for years.

Appetizers and Sandwiches

Helpful Hints

- Add flavor to tea by dissolving old-fashioned lemon drops or hard mint candies in it. They melt quickly and keep the tea brisk.

- Make your own spiced tea or cider. Place orange peels, whole cloves, and cinnamon sticks in a 6-inch square piece of cheesecloth. Gather the corners and tie with a string. Steep in hot cider or tea for 10 minutes; steep longer if you want a stronger flavor.

- Always chill juices or sodas before adding them to beverage recipes.

- Calorie-free club soda adds sparkle to iced fruit juices and reduces calories per portion.

- To cool your punch, float an ice ring made from the punch rather than using ice cubes. It appears more decorative, prevents diluting, and does not melt as quickly.

- Place fresh or dried mint in the bottom of a cup of hot chocolate for a cool and refreshing taste.

- When making fresh lemonade or orange juice, one lemon yields about ¼ cup juice, while one orange yields about ⅓ cup juice.

- Never boil coffee; it brings out acids and causes a bitter taste. Store ground coffee in the refrigerator or freezer to keep it fresh.

- Always use cold water for electric drip coffee makers. Use 1–2 tablespoons ground coffee for each cup of water.

- How many appetizers should you prepare? Allow 4–6 appetizers per guest if a meal quickly follows. If a late meal is planned, allow 6–8 appetizers per guest. If no meal follows, allow 8–10 pieces per guest.

- If serving appetizers buffet-style or seating is limited, consider no-mess finger foods that don't require utensils to eat.

- Think "outside the bowl." Choose brightly-colored bowls to set off dips or get creative with hollowed-out loaves of bread, bell peppers, heads of cabbage, or winter squash.

- Cheeses should be served at room temperature – approximately 70°.

- To keep appetizers hot, make sure you have enough oven space and warming plates to maintain their temperature.

- To keep appetizers cold, set bowls on top of ice or rotate bowls of dips from the fridge every hour or as needed.

Appetizers And Sandwiches

BOURBON GLAZED GEORGIA PECANS

2 c. Georgia pecan halves
4 oz. bourbon
¼ c. brown sugar
½ tsp. vanilla
¼ tsp. cinnamon
½ tsp. salt
Sugar (opt.)

In heavy skillet, combine pecans, bourbon, brown sugar, vanilla, cinnamon and salt. Cook over medium heat until caramelized. Spread evenly on cookie sheet and cool. If desired, when slightly warm, toss in sugar.

Note: A great way to greet your guests! They're so delicious you'll want to double the recipe!

OLIVE CHEESE DELIGHTS

1 c. shredded cheddar cheese
8 oz. cream cheese, softened
¼ c. finely chopped green olives with pimiento
¼ c. diced roasted red peppers
24 wonton skins
Vegetable oil

Blend cheddar cheese and cream cheese together in mixing bowl until smooth. Blend in olives and peppers. Divide mixture between wonton skins. Place in center of skins. Brush edges of skins with water and bring corners together to form a sack. Deep fry in vegetable oil until golden and crisp. Drain on paper towels.

Note: Have plenty on hand. These won't last! They freeze well too. Just let them set for 10 to 15 minutes after removing from freezer before frying.

PLANTATION CHEESEBALL

¼ c. finely minced onion
¼ c. finely minced bell pepper, red or green
2 T. margarine or butter
2 (8-oz.) pkgs. cream cheese, softened
1 (2-oz.) jar pimento peppers, drained
½ tsp. garlic powder
1 tsp. hot sauce
½ c. finely chopped pecans, toasted

Sauté onion and bell pepper in butter until tender. In mixing bowl, blend cream cheese with pimiento, garlic powder and hot sauce. Fold onion and pepper mixture into cheese. Shape into large ball and roll in toasted pecans until completely covered. Chill before serving.

Note: In the South, guests always enjoy a good chat and cocktails together before dinner. Try this delectable cheeseball at your next gathering.

LIVERWURST CHEESEBALL

4 oz. liverwurst
8 oz. cream cheese, softened
½ tsp. onion powder
½ tsp. garlic powder
½ tsp. black pepper
½ c. French-fried onions, crushed
3 T. bacon bits

In mixing bowl, combine liverwurst, cream cheese, onion powder, garlic powder and black pepper. Blend well. When thoroughly blended, form into a ball and roll in mixture of French-fried onions and bacon bits.

Note: Add whole wheat or rye crackers around this easy to prepare cheeseball. You'll make a bit at game time.

STRAWBERRY BLUSH CHEESEBALL

1 (8-oz.) pkg. cream cheese, softened
2 T. strawberry preserves
2 T. pink champagne
1 c. shredded Monterey Jack cheese
½ c. finely chopped, toasted almonds

Blend cream cheese with strawberry preserves and champagne. Next, blend in Monterey Jack cheese, mixing until smooth. Form into ball and roll in toasted almonds.

Note: Get off to a good start with the girls at a summer afternoon bridge game with this sparkling, fruity delight!

Key Lime Cheeseball

8-oz. pkg. cream cheese, softened
4 oz. shredded Jack cheese
½ tsp. Key lime zest
2 tsp. Key lime juice
½ tsp. sugar
¼ tsp. salt
½ c. toasted macadamia nuts, finely chopped

Thoroughly blend cream cheese and Jack cheese together. Add Key lime zest, lime juice, sugar and salt and continue to blend. Form into a ball and roll in macadamia nuts.

Note: If you're having a fish dinner, this is a great starter. Be sure to serve it at room temperature for the best flavor.

Georgia Cheese Ball

1 (8-oz.) pkg. cream cheese, softened
1 c. shredded Monterey Jack cheese
¼ c. coarsely chopped canned peaches
2 tsp. peach liqueur
½ c. toasted chopped pecans

Blend cream cheese and Jack cheese until smooth. Add peaches and peach liqueur and blend well. Form into round ball and roll in toasted nuts. Wrap in plastic wrap and refrigerate 2 to 4 hours or overnight.

Note: Serve this delicately flavored cheese ball with crackers at your next afternoon tea. You can omit the chopped pecans and use as a delicious filling for tea sandwiches.

Apple Cheeseball

1 lg. apple, peeled, cored and grated
1 T. lemon juice
1 c. shredded cheddar cheese
1 (8-oz.) pkg. cream cheese, softened
⅛ tsp. cinnamon
Dash salt
⅓ c. finely chopped walnuts, toasted

Toss grated apple with lemon juice. Cream cheddar cheese and cream cheese until smooth. Blend in apple, cinnamon and salt. Form into ball or log and roll in toasted nuts.

Note: A crackling fire and good friends is all it'll take to enjoy this delicious autumn favorite. Try serving with cheese or whole grain crackers.

LIVER 'N CHEESE PÂTÉ

8 oz. liverwurst
1 T. mayonnaise
½ tsp. ground red pepper
½ tsp. onion powder
4 oz. cream cheese, softened

Place liverwurst, mayonnaise, ground red pepper, onion powder and cream cheese in food processor. Blend 30 to 60 seconds or until creamy and smooth.

Note: Be sure to serve with a dark bread such as rye or pumpernickel. Makes an excellent filling for finger sandwiches on cocktail rye.

TAILGATE PASTRAMI BEER DIP

¼ lb. shaved pastrami, chopped
8 oz. cream cheese, softened
8 oz. grated Swiss cheese
½ c. beer
½ tsp. garlic powder

Combine pastrami, cream cheese, Swiss cheese and beer until smooth. Add garlic powder and blend.

Note: For the next big game, serve this with chips or fill baked potato skins.

SPICY SHRIMP DIP

1 (16-oz.) ctn. sour cream
½ c. mayonnaise
1 clove garlic, minced
2 tsp. cayenne pepper
½ tsp. Worcestershire sauce
½ tsp. salt
1 tsp. sugar
1 c. minced, cooked shrimp

In mixing bowl, blend sour cream and mayonnaise. Add garlic, cayenne pepper, Worcestershire sauce, salt and sugar. Blend well. Fold in shrimp. Cover and refrigerate until serving.

Note: This makes a perfect partner to crispy fried hush puppies. Try them at your next deck party.

SOUTHERN BLACK-EYED PEA LAYER DIP

2 T. oil
½ c. chopped Vidalia onion
¼ c. finely chopped celery
2 cloves garlic, minced
2 (15-oz.) cans black-eyed peas (1 drained, 1 undrained)
3 T. hot sauce
½ c. minced ham
1 c. shredded Pepper Jack cheese
1 c. fresh diced tomatoes
1 c. sour cream
½ c. chopped green onions

Heat oil in skillet and sauté onion, celery and garlic until tender. Stir in black-eyed peas, hot sauce and ham. Cook until heated through. In heatproof dish, layer pea mixture first. Follow with cheese, then tomatoes, sour cream and top with chopped green onions.

Note: A game time favorite!

DEEP SOUTH PULLED PORK BAR-B-QUE DIP

2 c. pulled, minced, cooked pork
½ c. hickory barbecue sauce
1 (8-oz.) can tomato sauce
2 med. tomatoes, diced
¼ c. sautéed chopped onion
2 tsp. hot sauce
½ tsp. garlic powder

In skillet, combine pork, barbecue sauce, tomato sauce, tomatoes, onion, hot sauce and garlic powder. Cook and simmer over low heat until hot. Serve very hot with corn chips.

Note: A summertime patio favorite! Transports well for "covered dish" parties too!

PECAN PRALINE CHEESE WHIP

8 oz. whipped cream cheese
1 tsp. brown sugar
1 T. butter
1 T. corn syrup
¼ c. toasted chopped pecans

In mixing bowl, blend cream cheese, brown sugar and butter. When blended, whip in corn syrup and fold in toasted pecans. Keep refrigerated.

Note: Delicious served on crackers or toast points but excellent for topping your baked sweet potato.

GEORGIA PEACHES 'N CREAM SPREAD

1 (8-oz.) can peaches in heavy
   syrup, drained
2 tsp. sugar

1 (8-oz.) pkg. cream cheese,
   softened
Assorted crackers

    Place drained peaches in processor and purée. Add sugar and cream cheese and pulse until smooth. Serve on crackers.

    Note: All that's missing is the rocking chair, mint julep and friends.

SOUTHERN PEANUT AND BACON SPREAD

¼ c. chopped onion
3 slices bacon, fried crisp and
   crumbled

8 oz. cream cheese, softened
2 T. chunky peanut butter
¼ tsp. salt

    Sauté onion in small amount of oil to golden and caramelized. Cool. Combine onion, bacon, cream cheese, peanut butter and salt until blended and of spreading consistency.

    Note: A wonderful filling for party sandwiches. Try it with apple slices for open face hors d'oeuvre.

NUTTY PICKLE RELISH SPREAD

⅔ c. chunky peanut butter
⅓ c. dill pickle relish

1 tsp. grated onion
1 T. toasted, chopped peanuts

    In bowl, blend peanut butter, dill pickle relish, onion and peanuts. Mix until well blended. Store covered in refrigerator.

    Note: Makes a delicious filling for tea sandwiches. Also excellent for school lunch sandwiches with potato chips.

Pumpkin Cheese Spread

2 (8-oz.) pkgs. cream cheese, softened
¾ c. canned pumpkin
¼ c. sugar
¼ tsp. salt
½ tsp. cinnamon
¼ tsp. nutmeg
½ tsp. vanilla
½ c. finely chopped toasted walnuts

In medium mixing bowl, combine cream cheese, pumpkin, sugar, salt, cinnamon, nutmeg and vanilla. Beat on medium speed with electric mixer until fluffy. Stir in walnuts. Store covered in refrigerator until ready to serve.

Note: You'll find this to be a very good "friend" to have on hand in the refrigerator during the festive fall and winter seasons. It's great on crackers, or for spreading on bread rounds. You'll find it's a big hit at breakfast with hot-from-the oven muffins.

Lemon Tuna Spread

1 (5-oz.) can solid albacore tuna, drained
4 oz. cream cheese, softened
1 tsp. finely grated lemon peel
1 T. mayonnaise
¼ tsp. garlic powder
Salt to taste

In mixing bowl, flake tuna. Add cream cheese and lemon peel and blend until smooth. Fold in mayonnaise and garlic powder. Add salt to taste. Keep refrigerated until ready to assemble sandwiches.

Note: A delicious sandwich filling but is delightful when used to stuff fresh garden tomatoes.

City Market Olive Spread

½ c. finely chopped green olives
⅓ c. mayonnaise
1 tsp. shredded lemon peel
1 clove garlic, finely minced
⅛ c. walnuts, finely chopped and toasted

Blend together olives, mayonnaise, lemon peel, garlic and walnuts. Mix until mixture is chunky smooth.

Note: Great on toasted bread rounds at cocktail time!

"SHRIMP BOAT" FINGER SANDWICHES

½ lb. cooked shrimp, finely chopped
1 clove garlic, minced
1 (8-oz.) pkg. cream cheese, softened
1 tsp. dill relish
Milk
1 (1-lb.) loaf white or wheat sandwich bread, crusts removed
Butter

Combine shrimp, garlic, cream cheese and relish until smooth, adding a few drops of milk, if needed, to make it spreading consistency. Lightly butter half of the bread slices, spread with cheese mixture and top with remaining slices. Cut each sandwich into 3 equal finger sandwiches.

Note: Serve these with sweet potato chips for a great afternoon snack at the boat house.

DAD'S SATURDAY AFTERNOON SANDWICHES

8 slices whole wheat bread
Mayonnaise
Mustard
4 slices cheddar cheese
4 slices garlic bologna
4 slices cotto salami
4 slices boiled ham
1 sm. onion, sliced paper thin
Hearts of 4 kosher dill pickles, sliced
1 vine-ripe tomato, sliced very thin

On 4 slices of bread, spread desired amount of mayonnaise. Repeat process with mustard on remaining 4 slices. On 4 slices with mayonnaise, place 1 slice each of cheddar cheese, bologna, salami and ham. Continue process with onion, pickle hearts and tomato. Top with mustard spread bread slices.

Note: I remember Dad making his famous sandwiches for our family on summer Saturday afternoons. It was always a treat for Mama and me before we left for an afternoon of shopping.

CELERY PEANUT FINGER SANDWICHES

1 (8-oz.) pkg. cream cheese, softened
¼ c. creamy peanut butter
¼ c. celery, finely minced
12 slices white sandwich bread, crusts removed
Softened butter
½ c. salted peanuts, finely chopped

Cream cream cheese and peanut butter together. Fold in celery. Assemble sandwiches by spreading 1½ to 2 tablespoons of filling on each of 6 slices. Top with remaining 6 slices. Cut each sandwich into 3 fingers. Spread softened butter lightly on both cut sides of finger sandwiches. Press in chopped peanuts to coat.

Note: At a spring afternoon tea, nothing will delight your guests like these delicate delicious tea sandwiches. They are beautiful on a sandwich plate and so refreshing when served slightly chilled.

AUTUMN APPLE-BACON SANDWICHES

2 med. apples, peeled, cored and sliced
4 T. butter
Cinnamon sugar
8 slices raisin bread
½ c. creamy peanut butter
8 slices breakfast bacon, fried crisp

Sauté apples in melted butter until tender crisp. Remove from pan, drain and sprinkle with cinnamon sugar. Set aside. Spread 4 slices of bread with half of peanut butter. Next layer with apple slices, then top with 2 slices of bacon per sandwich. Spread remaining slices of bread with remaining peanut butter and place on top.

Note: We first had these delightful sandwiches on a cold, crisp autumn day in Newport, RI. They are absolutely delicious with potato chips and a hot cup of tea.

PEPPER OLIVE TOASTED CHEESE SANDWICH

⅓ c. finely chopped green olives
⅓ c. finely chopped roasted red pepper
1 c. finely shredded sharp cheddar cheese
1 T. half-and-half
8 slices seeded rye sandwich bread
¼ c. margarine or butter

Combine olives, pepper and cheese together in mixing bowl. With fork, mix and blend together adding half-and-half and blending until of spreading consistency. Spread 4 slices of bread with cheese mixture, dividing equally between slices. Top with remaining 4 slices. Spread each side of sandwich with margarine and grill in skillet until golden brown on both sides.

Note: We like to serve a piping hot cup of tomato soup with these sandwiches. Makes a very nice lunch or simple supper by the fire.

RIVER STREET STUFFED SANDWICH WITH CREAMY ALE DRESSING

4 hoagie rolls
1 lb. med. shrimp, peeled
2 cloves minced garlic
4 tsp. diced roasted red pepper
2 T. butter or margarine
Salt and cayenne pepper to taste
1 c. Ale Dressing

Split hoagie rolls lengthwise and remove some of interior leaving a dish-like shell. Set aside. In skillet, place shrimp, garlic, red peppers and butter or margarine and sauté 5 minutes or until shrimp are pink. Season to taste with salt and pepper. Divide shrimp into 4 equal portions and fill rolls. Heavily drizzle each sandwich with Ale Dressing and serve cold or heated.

Ale Dressing:

⅓ c. mayonnaise
⅓ c. sour cream
⅓ c. ale
½ tsp. garlic powder
¼ tsp. sugar or to taste
¼ tsp. salt

Blend mayonnaise, sour cream, ale, garlic powder, sugar and salt until smooth and creamy.

Note: Serve these up with your favorite beer or sparkling ginger ale. Add some chips or a side of coleslaw and you've got a River Street feast!

Bourbon Peach Glazed Lil' Smokies

⅓ c. peach jam
3 T. bourbon

12 oz. cocktail-size smoked sausages

Heat jam in heavy skillet with bourbon on medium heat until saucy. Add sausages and cook until glazed.

Note: Keep it easy yet elegant with these little glazed sausages!

Patio Party Kabobs with Dipping Sauce

1 c. 1 inch cubed cantaloupe
1 c. 1 inch cubed ham
1 c. chunk pineapple
16 to 20 cherry tomatoes
1 c. sour cream
¼ c. mayonnaise

1 T. garlic powder
1 tsp. sugar
1 T. onion powder
1 tsp. salt
Milk

On 6- or 10-inch wooden skewers, alternately skewer on cantaloupe, ham, pineapple and cherry tomatoes in desired arrangement. Refrigerate until serving. Meanwhile for dipping sauce, combine sour cream, mayonnaise, garlic powder, sugar, onion powder and salt. When completely blended, add milk to desired consistency.

Note: For the busy hostess, make the dipping sauce 1 or 2 days ahead. Flavor improves with advance preparation.

Party Po' Boy

2 pt. oysters
1 c. buttermilk
3 T. hot sauce

1 lg. round loaf French bread
Oil
1½ c. cracker crumbs

Drain oysters; discard liquid. In small mixing bowl, combine buttermilk and hot sauce. Add oysters and let marinate 1 to 2 hours in refrigerator. Meanwhile, hollow bread loaf leaving 1½ inch wall and bottom. Set aside. Heat vegetable oil 1 inch deep in heavy skillet. Discard marinade from oysters. Dredge oysters in cracker crumbs and fry until golden. Remove from skillet and drain. Place oysters in bread bowl. Sprinkle all over with hot sauce and serve.

Note: Place this in the middle of your party buffet and watch them disappear!

CRISPY CORN PUPPIES

1¾ c. yellow cornmeal
½ c. flour
1 tsp. sugar
¾ tsp. baking soda
½ tsp. salt
¼ tsp. garlic powder
½ c. whole kernel corn, drained, reserved

¼ c. liquid
½ c. buttermilk
1 egg, beaten
1 c. finely crushed cornflakes
Oil for frying

In large bowl, sift together cornmeal, flour, sugar, baking soda, salt and garlic powder; blend well. Add corn and stir until well blended. In small bowl, combine reserved corn liquid, buttermilk and egg. Stir into dry ingredients and mix until all ingredients are blended. Drop by heaping teaspoon, one at a time, into cornflakes. (If dough is too soft to handle, add a little more cornmeal.) Roll to coat. Fry in 1 inch deep hot oil until golden brown turning once during frying. Remove and drain on paper towels.

Note: You'll find these crunchy corn puppies delightful served along with chowders or with fried fish and slaw. And they're great for a snack with your favorite dipping sauce.

SHRIMP PUPPIES

1¾ c. yellow cornmeal
½ c. flour
¾ tsp. sugar
¾ tsp. baking soda
¾ tsp. salt

½ tsp. garlic powder
½ c. chopped, cooked shrimp
1 c. buttermilk
1 egg, beaten
Oil for frying

In large mixing bowl, combine cornmeal, flour, sugar, baking soda, salt, garlic powder and shrimp. Mix well. Add buttermilk and egg. Stir until well blended and batter is moist. Heat oil in deep skillet and carefully drop batter by rounded teaspoons into hot oil. Fry until golden brown turning once while frying. Drain on paper towels.

Note: A Southern munchie that's guaranteed to please!

MUSHROOM PUFFS

1 (8-oz.) pkg. mushrooms
¼ c. salt pork, finely chopped
½ c. onion, chopped
Salt and pepper to taste
1 sheet frozen puff pastry, thawed
1 egg, beaten

Wash and chop mushrooms and set aside. Sauté salt pork and onions in small amount of oil until onions are transparent. Add mushrooms, salt and pepper. Sauté until mushrooms are tender. Roll pastry to ¹⁄₁₆ or ⅛ inch thick. Cut 24 (2-inch) rounds. Spoon about 2 teaspoons of filling onto 12 of the rounds. Place remaining 12 rounds on top and crimp edges together with fork. Place on baking sheet and brush with egg. Bake at 375° for 12 to 15 minutes or until medium golden brown.

Note: These versatile little puffs will be a hit at your next cocktail party or will beautifully compliment a roast beef dinner.

Recipe Favorites

Soups and Salads

Helpful Hints

- If the soup is not intended as the main course, count on 1 quart to serve 6. As the main dish, plan on 1 quart to serve 2.
- After cooking vegetables, pour any water and leftover vegetable pieces into a freezer container. When full, add tomato juice and seasoning to create a money-saving "free soup."
- Instant potatoes help thicken soups and stews.
- A leaf of lettuce dropped in a pot of soup absorbs grease from the top – remove the lettuce and serve. You can also make soup the day before, chill, and scrape off the hardened fat that rises to the top.
- To cut down on odors when cooking cabbage or cauliflower, add a little vinegar to the water and don't overcook.
- Three large stalks of celery, chopped and added to about two cups of beans (navy, brown, pinto, etc.), make the dish easier to digest.
- Fresh is best, but to reduce time in the kitchen, use canned or frozen broths or bouillon bases. Canned or frozen vegetables, such as peas, green beans, and corn, also work well.
- Ideally, cold soups should be served in chilled bowls.
- Perk up soggy lettuce by spritzing it with a mixture of lemon juice and cold water.
- You can easily remove egg shells from hard-boiled eggs if you quickly rinse the eggs in cold water after they are boiled. Add a drop of food coloring to help distinguish cooked eggs from raw ones.
- Your fruit salads will look better when you use an egg slicer to make perfect slices of strawberries, kiwis, or bananas.
- The ratio for a vinaigrette is typically 3 parts oil to 1 part vinegar.
- For salads, cook pasta al dente (slightly chewy to the bite). This allows the pasta to absorb some of the dressing and not become mushy.
- Fresh vegetables require little seasoning or cooking. If the vegetable is old, dress it up with sauces or seasoning.
- Chill the serving plates to keep the salad crisp.
- Fruit juices, such as pineapple and orange, can be used as salad dressing by adding a little olive oil, nutmeg, and honey.

Soups And Salads

GEORGIA PEANUT SOUP

2 (10¾-oz.) cans cream of celery soup
1½ c. half-and-half
⅓ c. creamy peanut butter
½ tsp. onion powder
¼ c. finely chopped roasted peanuts

In medium saucepan, combine celery soup with half-and-half whisking until smooth. Heat over medium heat 10 minutes. Stir in peanut butter and onion powder. Continue stirring until peanut butter is completely blended in. Simmer over low heat until hot. Serve topped with roasted peanuts.

Note: An old time favorite in the Deep South. It dates back to plantation days and is still a favorite at elegant dinners.

CHILLED PEAR SOUP

1 (15-oz.) can pears in fruit juice
¼ c. white wine
½ c. half-and-half
½ c. sour cream
Cinnamon

Drain pears, reserving juice. Purée pears in processor until smooth. In large mixing bowl, combine pear purée, reserved juice, white wine, half-and-half and sour cream. Blend with a whisk until thoroughly mixed. Chill in refrigerator 1 hour before serving. Before serving, whisk again. Lightly sprinkle cinnamon on top of each serving.

Note: A very delicate soup. Wonderful with deviled ham tea sandwiches at your next afternoon tea.

MARSHLAND CHICKEN AND WILD RICE SOUP

2 oz. salt pork, finely chopped
¼ c. finely chopped onion
2 (10¾-oz.) cans cream of chicken soup
2 c. half-and-half
½ tsp. ground red pepper
¼ tsp. salt
¼ tsp. black pepper
¼ tsp. ground sage
1 c. cooked wild rice

In large saucepan, sauté salt pork until golden. Add onions and sauté until tender. Whisk in chicken soup until blended. Slowly whisk in half-and-half. When smooth, stir in ground red pepper, salt, black pepper and sage. Stir in cooked wild rice. Let simmer 15 minutes before serving.

Note: Enjoy this satisfying hearty soup while sitting around a crackling fire with the family. It's great served with leftover buttermilk biscuits that are split, buttered and toasted in the oven.

SUMMERTIME CUCUMBER SOUP

2 lg. cucumbers, peeled and puréed
¼ c. white wine
1 c. sour cream
Salt to taste
White pepper to taste
½ tsp. onion powder
Fresh dill

In medium mixing bowl, combine cucumber, white wine, sour cream, salt, pepper and onion powder. Let stand in refrigerator 2 to 3 hours. Garnish with dill sprigs when serving.

Note: For those suffocatingly hot summer days that we have here in the South, this is a most welcomed treat. When served with a crisp chef's salad or finger sandwiches, it's the perfect way to cool off family and friends.

ORCHARD FRESH PEACH SOUP

2 fresh peaches, peeled, seeded and puréed
2 (8-oz.) ctn. peach yogurt
⅓ c. white wine
1 c. half-and-half
1 tsp. sugar (opt.)
Fresh sliced peaches for garnish

In medium bowl with wire whisk, combine peaches, yogurt, wine, half-and-half and sugar (optional). Blend well. Divide between serving dishes and garnish each serving with fresh peach slice.

Note: During peach season this is a good way to use those extra peaches. A delicious, cooling soup and so easy to prepare.

Summertime Peach Soup with Raspberry Creme

3 fresh peaches, peeled and finely chopped
1 c. peach nectar
⅓ c. peach wine
1 c. sour cream
⅔ c. half-and-half
1 (6-oz.) ctn. raspberry yogurt, stirred
Mint sprigs

In large bowl, combine peaches, nectar, wine, sour cream and half-and-half. Whisk until smooth and keep chilled until serving. When serving, into each bowl, swirl 1 tablespoon of raspberry yogurt and garnish with mint sprig.

Note: A simply delicious version of Georgia "peaches 'n cream."

Creamy Turnip Soup with Crispy Bacon Bits

6 slices bacon
2 c. cooked turnip roots, puréed
1 tsp. salt
1 c. heavy cream
1½ c. milk
1 T. butter

Fry bacon in skillet until crisp. Drain on paper towels and set aside. In saucepan, combine puréed turnip roots, salt, heavy cream and milk. Heat over medium heat. When hot, stir in butter until melted. Crumble bacon and top each serving of soup with bacon bits.

Note: Although this recipe was originally created in France many, many years ago it has long since been a favorite in the South.

Cream of Broccoli Soup

½ c. water
½ lb. broccoli flowerets
¼ c. chopped onion
¼ c. chopped celery
½ tsp. salt
1 (15-oz.) can cream of chicken soup

½ c. heavy cream
¾ c. milk
½ tsp. garlic powder
Salt and pepper to taste

Place water, broccoli, onion, celery and salt in 1-quart saucepan. Cook over medium heat until tender. In mixing bowl, whisk together chicken soup, heavy cream, milk and garlic powder until smooth. Add to cooked vegetable mixture in saucepan. Season with salt and pepper and heat over medium heat until heated thoroughly. Do not allow to boil.

Note: Soups are always a great starter for any meal. This soup can be used for a simple meal in your "everyday" dishes or at the beginning of an elegant dinner in your finest china.

Easy Pimiento Cheese Soup

2 (10¾-oz.) cans cheddar cheese soup
1 (2-oz.) jar diced pimiento, drained

1 c. half-and-half
1 c. milk
2 tsp. mayonnaise

In medium saucepan, combine cheese soup, diced pimiento, half-and-half, milk and mayonnaise. Whisk until smooth. Heat but do not let boil.

Note: So easy but so good! Serve with tea sandwiches at high tea.

DEEP SOUTH CREAM OF LIMA BEAN SOUP

2 T. butter
¼ c. chopped onion
¼ c. chopped red bell pepper
2 (15-oz.) cans lima beans, undrained
¼ tsp. salt
¼ tsp. black pepper
1½ c. half-and-half
½ c. heavy cream

In medium saucepan, melt butter. Sauté onion and bell pepper until tender. Add lima beans, salt and pepper. Let heat over medium heat for 15 minutes. Slowly whisk in half-and-half and heavy cream. Continue to heat for 15 minutes longer not allowing it to boil. Serve with toasted Ham Croutons.

Ham Croutons:

1 c. ham, cut in ¼-inch cubes
3 tsp. oil (add more, if needed)

In skillet, heat oil, add ham and sauté until brown and crispy. Drain on paper towels.

Note: Monday was always wash day so lima bean soup for supper was a big help. Now we have automatic washers and time saving recipes such as this one. Just look at the time you'll have left over.

SOUTHERN CREAM OF COLLARD SOUP

2 oz. salt pork, finely chopped
¼ c. finely chopped onion
2 c. cooked collard greens, puréed
1 c. chicken broth
1 tsp. sugar
1 T. hot pepper vinegar
Salt to taste
½ c. heavy cream

In large saucepan, sauté salt pork until golden. Add onions and sauté until tender. Whisk in collard purée and chicken broth until well blended. Stir in sugar and hot pepper vinegar. Season with salt. Simmer for 20 minutes. Before serving, slowly add cream and allow to heat but not boil.

Note: A velvety soup that is oh, so satisfying! Try it with sandwiches for a luncheon or my favorite way, as a side to a meatless supper of mac 'n cheese, sliced tomatoes and crispy fried okra.

SUMMERTIME BLACKBERRY SOUP

2 (8-oz.) ctn. blackberry yogurt
¼ c. sour cream
⅓ c. blackberry wine
1 c. half-and-half
1 tsp. sugar (opt.)
½ c. fresh blackberries

In large mixing bowl with wire whisk, blend yogurt, sour cream and wine. Blend well. Slowly add half-and-half and sugar (optional), whisking to blend. Keep chilled until serving time. Garnish each serving with 2 or 3 berries.

Note: Another Southern favorite in the summertime!

PLANTATION CREAMY BLACK-EYED PEA SOUP WITH PIMIENTO PEPPER PURÉE

2 oz. salt pork, finely chopped
½ c. finely chopped onion
2 (15-oz.) cans black-eyed peas, undrained
1 (15-oz.) can chicken broth
½ c. heavy cream
Salt and pepper to taste
Pimiento pepper purée

In large saucepan, sauté pork until golden. Add onion and sauté until tender. Stir in black-eyed peas. Next, blend in chicken broth and heavy cream. Add salt and pepper to taste. Simmer over low heat for 20 minutes not allowing it to boil. Ladle into bowls and top with 1 tablespoon of pimiento pepper purée in center.

Pimiento Pepper Purée:

1 (2-oz.) jar pimiento peppers, puréed
2 T. hot pepper vinegar
1 tsp. brown sugar

Combine puréed pimiento, pepper vinegar and brown sugar until well blended.

Note: A cup of this creamy soup served before a southern fried chicken dinner is Deep South eatin' at its best!

Mama's Shrimp Bisque

2 T. margarine
¼ c. finely chopped red bell pepper
1 clove garlic, minced
¼ lb. salad shrimp
2 (15-oz.) cans cream of tomato soup
1½ c. milk
½ c. heavy cream
Salt to taste

Melt margarine in large saucepan. Sauté red pepper until tender. Add garlic and shrimp and sauté 2 to 3 minutes. Blend in tomato soup. Whisk in milk until smooth. Stir in heavy cream and add salt to taste. Heat on low heat 10 to 15 minutes not allowing it to boil. Serve hot.

Note: For a working mom or any mom, this is an easy way to prepare a starter for dinner or a hearty lunch.

Summer Squash Bisque

2 T. margarine
½ c. finely chopped onion
2 c. sliced yellow squash
2 c. chicken stock
1 c. half-and-half
¼ c. heavy cream
½ c. shredded Pepper Jack cheese
½ tsp. paprika
½ tsp. salt

In large saucepan, melt margarine. Sauté onion and squash together until tender. Remove from heat. Cool slightly. Purée in processor until smooth. Return to saucepan and over medium heat add chicken stock. Whisk in half-and-half and heavy cream until thoroughly blended. Simmer for 10 minutes. Add cheese, paprika and salt. Stir until cheese is melted. Heat thoroughly before serving.

Note: The perfect match for ham sandwiches.

TYBEE CREAMY SEAFOOD BISQUE

2 T. margarine
3 oz. shrimp, peeled, deveined and chopped
3 oz. bay scallops, chopped
1 (10¾-oz.) can cream of onion soup
¼ c. white wine
¼ c. heavy cream
1 c. milk
1 tsp. parsley flakes
½ tsp. dried tarragon
¾ tsp. paprika
½ tsp. garlic powder

Melt margarine in large saucepan. Sauté shrimp and scallops 2 to 3 minutes. Add cream of onion soup. Whisk in white wine until smooth. Next, whisk in heavy cream, then milk. When thoroughly combined, stir in parsley, tarragon, paprika and garlic powder. Let simmer over low heat for 20 to 30 minutes not allowing it to boil.

Note: Serving bisque is an excellent way to start a meal. This hearty recipe can stand alone when served with crusty bread and butter and a salad.

SKIDAWAY ISLAND CORN AND CRAB CHOWDER

2 T. butter
¼ c. diced salt pork
⅓ c. green bell pepper, chopped
1 sm. onion, finely chopped
1 (15-oz.) can whole kernel corn
1 (15-oz.) can cream-style corn
1 c. lump crabmeat (fresh or canned)
¼ c. heavy cream
1½ c. half-and-half
Salt and pepper to taste

Melt butter in heavy saucepan and sauté salt pork until beginning to brown. Add bell pepper and onion and sauté until tender. Add whole kernel corn, cream-style corn and crabmeat. Blend together then stir in heavy cream and half-and-half and season with salt and pepper to taste. Let simmer on low heat for 30 minutes. Serve with crispy okra croutons.

Note: This recipe was inspired by a chowder we once had while crusin' the Old Mississippi. Be sure to have hot hard rolls and a tub of sweet butter to top off this old Southern favorite.

Low Country Cioppino

¼ c. cubed salt pork
Oil
1 red bell pepper
1 green bell pepper
¼ c. chopped celery
1 clove garlic, crushed
1 med. onion, finely chopped
1 (15-oz.) can diced, stewed tomatoes
1 (8-oz.) can tomato sauce
¾ c. water
1 lb. raw med. shrimp, peeled and deveined
½ doz. raw oysters
1 c. flaked crabmeat

Sauté salt pork in small amount of oil in large Dutch oven. When partially done, add peppers, celery, garlic and onion. Cook until onions are translucent. Add tomatoes and tomato sauce along with the water. Let simmer 10 minutes. Add shrimp, oysters and crabmeat and cook over medium heat about 10 minutes or until shrimp are pink and oysters are curled. Serve in bowls over yellow rice accompanied by hot crusty bread.

Note: Fresh baked bread hot from the oven, sweet butter and crisp salad makes this Low Country Cioppino a hearty, pleasing supper.

River Street Oyster Stew

2 slices bacon, chopped
½ c. chopped onion
⅓ c. chopped celery
2 T. butter or margarine
1 pt. oysters, undrained
⅓ c. white wine
⅓ c. chopped roasted red pepper
½ tsp. ground red pepper
1¾ c. milk
1 c. heavy cream
Salt and pepper to taste

Sauté bacon, onion and celery in butter or margarine until tender. Add oysters and white wine, roasted red pepper and ground red pepper. Cook until oysters curl. Add milk and cream. Season with salt and pepper and heat until hot not allow to boil.

Note: This is best when served on a cold winter night...it's even better if you can wait until it's raining!

MRS. RABBIT'S WINTER CARROT STEW

⅓ c. finely chopped salt pork
1 med. onion, finely chopped
2 (15-oz.) can sliced carrots, undrained
1 (15-oz.) can chicken broth
1 (15-oz.) can chicken gravy
Black pepper to taste

Sauté salt pork until tender. Add onions and sauté until tender and translucent. Add carrots and cook 5 minutes. Add chicken broth and gravy. Stir until smooth. Add pepper to taste. Cook 10 minutes or until heated thoroughly.

Note: The whimsical name for this recipe is an old family fable. It was created to entice little ones to eat their vegetables.

CHEDDAR PASTA WALDORF SALAD

3 c. cooked salad pasta, drained
2 lg. apples, peeled, cored and cubed
¾ c. finely shredded cheddar cheese
½ c. raisins
⅓ c. mayonnaise
⅓ c. sour cream
½ c. chopped walnuts, toasted
Salt to taste

In a large mixing bowl, combine pasta, apples, cheese and raisins. Toss until blended. Fold in mayonnaise and sour cream. Mix well then add walnuts and salt. Fold until blended well. Chill until serving.

Note: Try serving this delightful salad with finger sandwiches and a cup of soup at your next ladies' luncheon. It's a nice twist on an old favorite.

SOUTHERN TURNIP SALAD

3 c. cubed, cooked turnip roots
¼ c. diced onion
½ c. finely chopped pickled okra
3 strips bacon, fried crisp and crumbled
3 to 4 T. sour cream
¼ tsp. cayenne pepper
½ tsp. black pepper
½ to ¾ tsp. sugar
½ tsp. salt

In large mixing bowl, combine turnip roots, onion, pickled okra and bacon; gently toss together. Add sour cream, cayenne, black pepper, sugar and salt. Fold in until well mixed as you would for potato salad. Chill or serve at room temperature.

Note: A nice change from potato salad. Goes very well with barbecued pork or chicken.

Houseboat Turnip Salad

3 c. cooked, cubed turnip roots
¼ c. chopped red onion
3 green onions, chopped
6 slices bacon, fried crisp and crumbled
2 T. rice vinegar
1 T. oil
1 T. sugar
2 tsp. diced pimiento
¼ tsp. salt
¼ tsp. black pepper

In mixing bowl, combine turnips, red onion, green onion and bacon. Set aside. In measuring cup, blend vinegar, oil, sugar, pimiento, salt and pepper. Drizzle over salad mixture and toss. Let marinate several hours before serving. If you want a saucier salad, double the amounts of the dressing.

Note: Along the riverbanks in the South are many homesteads with gardens near the river's edge. Turnips and onions are Southern favorites and this delicious salad is a favorite of river folk. Serve with crispy fried catfish, corn pone and sliced tomatoes.

Chicken Pecan Salad

2 c. diced, cooked chicken
⅓ c. chopped, toasted pecans
⅛ c. grated Parmesan cheese
½ tsp. fresh grated lemon peel
1 clove garlic, finely minced
4 T. mayonnaise
½ tsp. black pepper

In medium mixing bowl, combine chicken, pecans, Parmesan, lemon peel and garlic. Toss and mix well. Add mayonnaise and black pepper and continue mixing until well blended. Chill until serving.

Note: A most versatile salad. Can be used for sandwiches, as a spread on party crackers or a delicious filling for stuffed tomatoes.

CITRUS CHICKEN SALAD

2 c. chopped, cooked chicken breast
¼ c. chopped toasted pecans
¼ c. diced water chestnuts
¼ c. chopped onion
½ c. chopped celery
Salt and pepper to taste
½ c. mayonnaise
¼ c. sour cream
1 c. mandarin orange segments, drained
½ c. green grapes

In large mixing bowl, combine chicken, pecans, water chestnuts, onion, celery, salt and pepper. Toss gently. Add mayonnaise and sour cream. Blend thoroughly. Fold in orange segments and grapes. Chill until ready to serve.

Note: A great dish for a luncheon on a hot summer afternoon.

CRISPY CHICKEN SALAD

2 c. cubed, cooked chicken breast
¼ c. finely chopped bell pepper
¼ c. finely chopped onion
3 T. dill relish
⅓ c. mayonnaise
⅓ c. sour cream
½ c. plus ¼ c. canned French-fried onions

In medium mixing bowl, blend chicken, bell pepper and onion together. Fold in relish, mayonnaise and sour cream. Toss in ½ cup French-fried onions. Mix well. When serving, top with remaining ¼ cup French-fried onions.

Note: With that leftover chicken, you can prepare this delightful salad for a quick lunch.

SPRINGTIME JELLIED CHICKEN SALAD

2 c. clear chicken broth
1 env. unflavored gelatin
¼ c. minced green pepper
2 T. minced pimiento
¼ c. minced onion

1 c. finely minced, cooked chicken
½ tsp. salt
½ tsp. white pepper
1 T. lemon juice
Oil

Place ¼ cup chicken broth in small saucepan. Sprinkle gelatin over surface. Let stand until gelatin is softened, about 10 minutes. In large mixing bowl, combine green pepper, pimiento, onion, chicken, salt and pepper. Mix until blended and set aside. Over low heat, stir gelatin mixture until gelatin dissolves. Add to remaining chicken broth along with lemon juice. Pour broth mixture over chicken mixture and stir until blended. Very lightly grease a 2-cup mold. Pour into mold and chill until firm, 3 to 4 hours or overnight.

Note: On those hot Southern summer days, serve this spicy and cooling loaf with your favorite potato salad, sliced tomatoes and Southern Sweet Tea.

TURKEY CITRUS SALAD

⅓ c. mayonnaise
⅓ c. sour cream
2 T. orange juice
1½ c. cubed, cooked turkey breast
⅓ c. dried cranberries

1 c. orange segments
⅓ c. chopped celery
¼ c. chopped walnuts, toasted
Salt and pepper to taste

In small bowl, blend mayonnaise, sour cream and orange juice. Set aside. In large bowl, combine turkey, cranberries, oranges, celery and walnuts. Toss until mixed well. Gently fold in mayonnaise mixture until blended. Season with salt and pepper. Chill before serving.

Note: Treat the girls to a special salad at bridge. You can prepare this a day in advance. Keep covered in refrigerator until needed. Dishes like this gives you more time to be a gracious hostess!

Low Country Potato Salad

4 med. potatoes, peeled, cubed, boiled and drained
1 sm. onion, chopped
¼ c. chopped celery
4 T. dill relish
½ c. mayonnaise
2 T. sugar
⅓ c. canned whole kernel corn, drained
½ c. sliced, cooked okra
¼ lb. cooked smoked sausage, sliced thin

In large mixing bowl, combine potatoes, onion and celery. Add relish, mayonnaise and sugar. Mix thoroughly. Fold in corn, okra and sausage. Let stand in refrigerator 4 to 6 hours or overnight so flavors can blend.

Note: This is a "loaded" potato salad with a low country flair. Excellent with hot fried chicken or crispy fried fish. The secret to its flavor is in preparing it several hours or the day before serving.

Stateline Citrus-Shrimp Salad

4 c. salad greens mix
2 c. fresh Florida orange sections
2 c. fresh Florida grapefruit sections
½ lb. sautéed med. Georgia shrimp, peeled
1 sm. red onion, thinly sliced
½ c. candied pecans
1 c. orange juice
⅛ c. vinegar
1 T. salad oil
2 T. sugar

Divide salad greens between 4 salad plates. Arrange orange and grapefruit sections in circular pattern. Place shrimp in center. Top with onion rings and sprinkle with candied pecans. In small mixing bowl, combine orange juice, vinegar, oil and sugar. Mix well and splash over salads.

Note: Florida citrus and Georgia shrimp meet in this "stateline" salad. It's a most attractive dish because of its vibrant colors.

River's Edge Roasted Potato Salad

1½ lbs. new red potatoes, quartered and boiled until tender crisp, drained
4 T. melted margarine
2 cloves garlic, minced
¾ tsp. sea salt
1 T. yellow mustard
1 T. vegetable oil
⅓ c. bleu cheese dressing
½ c. salsa (mild or hot)
2 eggs, hard boiled, grated
⅓ c. shredded Jack cheese
2 slices bacon, fried and crumbled

Place drained potatoes on buttered baking sheet. Drizzle with melted margarine and sprinkle with half the garlic and salt. Roast in oven at 450° for 20 minutes or until golden, tossing frequently until tender. In small bowl, combine mustard and oil. Add remaining garlic and bleu cheese. In large bowl, place potatoes and toss with dressing mixture. Spoon salsa over top. Sprinkle with grated egg and cheese and top with crumbled bacon.

Note: Take along when going to the river for the day. Delicious with fresh caught fried trout!

Roasted Red Pepper Potato Salad

4 c. cubed red potatoes, unpeeled and cooked until tender, drained
½ c. chopped roasted red pepper
1 clove garlic, chopped
½ c. mayonnaise
½ c. sour cream
1 T. sugar
1 tsp. salt
1 tsp. black pepper
1 T. dried parsley flakes

In large mixing bowl, place potatoes, red pepper and garlic. Mix. Fold in mayonnaise, sour cream, sugar, salt and pepper. Blend well. Place in serving bowl and sprinkle top with parsley flakes. Chill.

Note: Take this salad to your next pot luck. Everyone will rave over it.

ℛIVERBOAT SWEET CORN POTATO SALAD

4 c. cubed, cooked new potatoes, skin on
1 c. canned whole kernel corn, drained
4 green onions, chopped
2 cloves garlic, minced

⅓ c. mayonnaise
⅓ c. sour cream
2 T. yellow mustard
4 T. honey
¼ tsp. salt
½ tsp. black pepper

In large mixing bowl, combine potatoes, corn, onions and garlic and toss. In separate bowl, blend mayonnaise, sour cream, mustard, honey, salt and pepper. Blend well and fold into potato-corn mixture. Mix well and let stand 4 hours or more in refrigerator before serving.

Note: This recipe was inspired by a salad we once had on board an old Southern paddle wheeler. It is a perfect side to fried chicken and baked beans. Add iced tea, chocolate cake and ice cold watermelon and your set for a day of river cruising.

ℋAM SALAD STUFFED TOMATOES

4 lg. fresh tomatoes
1½ c. finely minced ham
1½ T. chopped peanuts
2 T. minced dill pickles

3 T. minced onion
¼ c. mayonnaise
Paprika
Parsley snips

Wash and dry tomatoes. With sharp knife starting at center, cut into quarters or eighths ¾ of way down. Pull gently apart. Set aside. In mixing bowl, combine ham, peanuts, pickles, onion and mayonnaise. Blend very well. Divide equally among the 4 tomatoes. Sprinkle with paprika and garnish with parsley.

Note: Try this tasty and colorful luncheon favorite on a spring day after gardening.

ℳELON COCKTAIL SALAD

3 c. seedless watermelon balls
1 c. seedless green grapes
3 c. cantaloupe balls

1 c. pitted Bing cherries
2 T. sugar
1½ c. pink champagne

In large mixing bowl, combine watermelon, grapes, cantaloupe and cherries. Stir sugar into champagne and pour over fruit. Toss lightly and chill until serving.

Note: For the most elegant presentation of this summertime salad, serve in champagne flutes or any stemmed cocktail glass.

Summer Melon Salad

4 c. 1-inch cube seedless watermelon
1 c. seedless red grapes
⅓ c. chopped green onions
⅓ c. chopped, toasted walnuts or pecans
½ c. crumbled feta cheese
½ c. vinaigrette dressing

In large salad bowl, gently toss melon cubes, grapes, onions and walnuts or pecans. Sprinkle feta cheese over top of salad and serve vinaigrette on side or drizzle over top.

Vinaigrette Dressing:

4 T. rice vinegar
⅛ c. water
1 tsp. salad oil
2½ T. sugar
½ tsp. salt

Whisk vinegar, water and oil together. Stir in sugar until dissolved. Add salt and mix well. Chill until serving time.

Note: For a less casual presentation, divide salad into salad plates before adding the feta cheese. Top each salad with feta cheese and pass vinaigrette when serving.

Strawberry-Peach Cream Parfaits

1 c. sour cream
⅛ c. sugar
1½ c. sweetened, sliced strawberries
1½ c. sliced peaches
¼ c. light brown sugar
Whipped topping
Fresh mint sprigs
Strawberry halves

In bowl, combine sour cream and sugar. Mix until sugar is dissolved. In parfait glasses, begin layering with strawberries, then peaches. Next, sprinkle with brown sugar, then a layer of sour cream mixture. Repeat process until glasses are filled. Finish with a dollop of whipped topping, a sprig of mint and a strawberry half.

Note: This lovely summer treat is as attractive as it is delicious. It can be served as a salad or a dessert. It can even be that special added touch to a summer afternoon tea.

GEORGIA PEACH SALAD

4 lg. fresh peaches, peeled and
   sliced
4 T. lemon juice
1 c. green grapes
¼ c. chopped celery
½ c. sour cream
2 T. sugar
½ tsp. vanilla

In salad bowl, toss peaches in lemon juice. Add grapes and celery. In small mixing bowl, blend sour cream, sugar and vanilla until thoroughly mixed. Spoon over fruit in bowl and toss to evenly coat. Chill.

Note: Enjoy this salad as a prelude to a delicious baked ham dinner.

BLEU CHEESE AND WALNUT STUFFED PEAR SALAD

2 lg. Bartlett pears, cored and
   halved
3 T. lemon juice
¼ c. crumbled bleu cheese
¼ c. toasted, chopped walnuts
1½ T. mayonnaise
1 T. sour cream
Mint for garnish

Scoop pulp from pear halves leaving a ¼-inch shell. Completely brush pear shell with lemon juice to prevent darkening. Toss removed pear pulp with lemon juice and combine with bleu cheese, walnuts, mayonnaise and sour cream. Spoon mixture into pear shells, garnish with sprig of mint and chill until serving.

Note: For that special tea, serve this lovely and delectable salad to accompany ham tea sandwiches.

Tomato and Brussels Sprout Salad

1 (10-oz.) pkg. frozen Brussels
   sprouts
1 c. cherry tomato halves
½ c. thinly sliced red onion
⅓ c. grated carrot
4 T. dill relish
½ c. dill vinaigrette

Cook Brussels sprouts according to package directions. Drain and let cool. In large mixing bowl, combine sprouts, tomatoes, onion, carrot and relish. Toss well. Drizzle with vinaigrette and toss again. Chill before serving.

Dill Vinaigrette:

½ c. dill pickle juice
1 T. lemon juice
1 clove garlic, minced
2 T. oil
2 tsp. sugar

In small bowl, whisk together pickle juice, lemon juice, garlic, oil and sugar. Whisk until well blended. Refrigerate until ready to use.

Note: Very tasty with Mustard Crusted Pepper Coated Ham Steaks. It can be made a day in advance for the best flavor.

Southern Squash Salad

3 c. baked squash (acorn, or
   butternut), cubed
¼ c. finely chopped onion
¼ c. finely chopped celery
3 T. dill relish
3 to 4 T. mayonnaise
1 tsp. sugar
¾ tsp. salt
¾ tsp. black pepper

In large mixing bowl, combine squash, onion, celery, relish, mayonnaise, sugar, salt and pepper. Blend together as you would for potato salad. Chill until serving.

Note: For a pleasant change from potato salad, serve this with smoked sausage and buttered corn.

WILMINGTON ISLAND SALMON SALAD

1½ c. uncooked salad pasta
⅓ c. sour cream
½ c. mayonnaise
½ tsp. minced garlic
1 T. lemon juice
1 tsp. lemon rind, grated
1½ tsp. dried dill
⅔ c. drained, flaked canned salmon
Salt and pepper
Lemon slices

Cook pasta according to package directions and drain. In large mixing bowl, add sour cream, mayonnaise, garlic, lemon juice, lemon rind and dill. Mix until well blended. Fold in salmon and season with salt and pepper to taste. Garnish with lemon slices when serving.

Note: After a day at the beach enjoy this refreshing salmon salad. It's easy to make a day ahead giving you more leisure time.

COUNTRY HARVEST APPLE SALAD

3 lg. apples, peeled, cored and chunked
⅓ c. raisins, soaked in water until plump
⅓ c. mayonnaise
⅓ c. chunky peanut butter
¼ tsp. salt

Combine apples and drained raisins in mixing bowl. In separate bowl, blend mayonnaise and peanut butter until well blended. Add to apple raisin mixture along with salt and toss until well coated.

Note: On a crisp autumn day this is delicious served with cheese tea sandwiches and hot tea or to accompany roasted wieners and baked beans for a fireside get-to-gether.

SUMMER PEPPER SALAD

1 (16-oz.) jar roasted red peppers
1 sm. onion, thinly sliced
½ c. sliced ripe olives
1 med. cucumber, peeled and sliced thin
¼ c. white vinegar
1 T. oil
2 T. water
2 T. sugar
½ tsp. salt

Strip peppers into ¼-inch strips. Place in salad bowl. Add onions, olives and cucumber. In separate container, combine vinegar, oil, water, sugar and salt. Pour over salad and let marinate 2 to 3 hours before serving.

Note: A very versatile salad with a lot of flavor. It can accompany most any main dish from roast beef to fried seafood.

COUNTRY-STYLE BEET SALAD

1 (15-oz.) can pickled beets, julienned
2 T. sugar
1 lg. Granny Smith apple, peeled and diced
¼ c. chopped onion

In mixing bowl, combine beets and sugar. Stir until dissolved. Add apple and onions. Combine well. Chill until served.

Note: Home grown pickled beets makes this recipe even tastier.

SAVORY CREAMED BEET AND APPLE SALAD

1 (15-oz.) can shoestring beets, drained
1 med. apple, peeled and cubed
1 sm. white onion, thinly sliced
2 T. vinegar
3 T. sugar
½ tsp. salt
½ tsp. oil
½ c. sour cream
1 clove garlic, crushed
½ tsp. caraway seed

In mixing bowl, toss beets, apple and onion. Stir in vinegar, sugar, salt and oil. Set aside. In small bowl, blend sour cream, garlic and caraway seed. Fold gently into beet and apple mixture. Chill until serving.

Note: A delicious salad to serve with corned beef or smoked sausage.

LOW COUNTRY CREAMY SLAW

½ c. mayonnaise
¼ c. sour cream
4 T. dill pickle relish
½ tsp. ground red pepper
1 (1-lb.) pkg. shredded coleslaw mix
1 sm. onion, finely chopped
¼ lb. cooked salad shrimp
Salt and pepper

In medium mixing bowl, combine mayonnaise, sour cream, relish and ground red pepper. Fold in coleslaw mix and onion. Mix until creamy and coated. then fold in shrimp. Season with salt and pepper to taste. Chill and serve.

Note: For a quick, light lunch, this salad can stand alone when served with crackers or Wheat Thins.

CRISP ICEBERG WEDGES WITH CREAMY SLAW DRESSING

1 head chilled, crisp iceberg
   lettuce, washed
1 c. mayonnaise
¼ c. dill relish
1 tsp. onion powder

1 tsp. sugar
1 T. prepared mustard
¼ tsp. salt
2 T. lemon juice

Cut lettuce into 6 wedges, rinse each wedge well under water. Drain and set aside. In mixing bowl whisk together mayonnaise, relish, onion powder, sugar, mustard, salt and lemon juice until smooth. Chill until serving. To serve, top each wedge with generous amount of dressing.

Note: I remember my grandmother serving this "salad" at summer lunches. It's simple, delicious and so attractive.

LEMON SLAW

3 c. shredded cabbage
¼ c. diced onion
3 T. diced pimiento
3 T. dill relish
1 T. grated lemon peel
10 paper-thin lemon slices, cut in
   halves

½ c. mayonnaise
3 T. sugar or to taste
2 T. lemon juice
1 tsp. salt
½ tsp. black pepper

In large mixing bowl, combine cabbage, onion, pimiento, relish and lemon peel. Toss until mixed. Add ⅔ of lemon slices, mayonnaise, sugar, lemon juice, salt and pepper. Toss well. When serving, garnish with ⅓ remaining lemon slices.

Note: A refreshingly tangy slaw. Great with fish or seafood.

JEWELED RICE SALAD

¼ c. orange juice
2 T. salad oil
3 T. rice vinegar
2½ c. cooked yellow rice
⅓ c. dried cranberries

½ c. mandarin orange segments
¼ c. chopped, toasted walnuts
⅓ c. chopped red onion
⅓ c. chopped celery
Salt to taste

In small bowl, blend orange juice, oil and rice vinegar together. Set aside. In medium salad bowl, toss rice, cranberries, orange segments, walnuts, onion and celery. When thoroughly tossed, sprinkle with salt to taste. Drizzle dressing over rice mixture and toss to blend.

Note: A colorful side to accent Blackberry Glazed Chicken Breasts!

Recipe Favorites

Helpful Hints

- When preparing a casserole, make an additional batch to freeze for when you're short on time. Use within 2 months.
- To keep hot oil from splattering, sprinkle a little salt or flour in the pan before frying.
- To prevent pasta from boiling over, place a wooden spoon or fork across the top of the pot while the pasta is boiling.
- Boil all vegetables that grow above ground without a cover.
- Never soak vegetables after slicing; they will lose much of their nutritional value.
- Green pepper may change the flavor of frozen casseroles. Clove, garlic, and pepper flavors get stronger when frozen, while sage, onion, and salt become more mild.
- For an easy no-mess side dish, grill vegetables along with your meat.
- Store dried pasta, rice (except brown rice), and whole grains in tightly covered containers in a cool, dry place. Refrigerate brown rice and freeze grains if you will not use them within 5 months.
- A few drops of lemon juice added to simmering rice will keep the grains separated.
- When cooking greens, add a teaspoon of sugar to the water to help vegetables retain their fresh colors.
- To dress up buttered, cooked vegetables, sprinkle them with toasted sesame seeds, toasted chopped nuts, canned french-fried onions, grated cheese, or slightly crushed seasoned croutons.
- Soufflé dishes are designed with straight sides to help your soufflé rise. Ramekins work well for single-serve casseroles.
- A little vinegar or lemon juice added to potatoes before draining will make them extra white when mashed.
- To avoid toughened beans or corn, add salt midway through cooking.
- If your pasta sauce seems a little dry, add a few tablespoons of the pasta's cooking water.
- To prevent cheese from sticking to a grater, spray the grater with cooking spray before beginning.

Copyright © Morris Press Cookbooks

Vegetables And Sides

SUNDAY AFTERNOON DEVILED EGGS

6 lg. eggs, hard boiled and peeled
4 oz. cream cheese, softened
3 tsp. mayonnaise
¼ c. shredded cheddar cheese
1 T. minced celery
2 tsp. minced onion
½ tsp. prepared yellow mustard

Slice eggs in half lengthwise and remove yolks. Set whites aside. Blend yolks with cream cheese and mayonnaise until smooth. Add cheddar cheese, celery, onion and mustard. Blend until fluffy. Spoon mixture into egg whites.

Note: At any Sunday dinner at Grandma's house, we were sure to find a beautiful platter of deviled eggs. No Sunday dinner in the South is complete without 'em!

ZESTY DEVILED EGGS

6 lg. eggs, hard boiled, peeled and halved
1 T. finely chopped green onion
1 T. finely chopped red bell pepper
1 tsp. chopped jalapeños
1 T. mayonnaise
1 tsp. yellow mustard
¼ tsp. garlic powder
⅛ tsp. salt
Parsley
Paprika

Remove yolks from egg white. Mash yolks with fork until creamy. Add green onions, red pepper, jalapeños, mayonnaise, mustard, garlic powder and salt. Blend until smooth. Divide mixture evenly between egg whites. Top with sprinkling of paprika and sprig of parsley.

Note: Don't forget a plate of these for the picnic basket! You can double or triple the recipe for a really large gathering. Make them the day before and store in an airtight container in the fridge.

"EGG SALAD" DEVILED EGGS

6 hard-boiled eggs, peeled and halved lengthwise
3 hard-boiled eggs, peeled
3 T. mayonnaise
¼ tsp. Creole seasoning
2 heaping tsp. grated onion
⅛ tsp. garlic powder
1½ tsp. dill relish
⅛ tsp. salt or to taste
Paprika
Parsley sprigs

Remove yolks from split eggs and place in mixing bowl. Finely chop 3 peeled eggs and add to yolks. with fork, blend egg yolks into finely chopped eggs. Stir in mayonnaise, Creole seasoning, grated onion, garlic powder, relish and salt. Blend until creamy. Divide between egg white halves mounding, if necessary. Garnish with paprika and parsley sprigs.

Note: A picnic favorite and oh so yummy!

FRIED GREEN TOMATOES WITH HOT CREAMY ONION SAUCE

3 lg. green tomatoes, sliced ¼ inch thick
½ c. buttermilk
¼ c. flour
½ c. yellow cornmeal
½ tsp. salt
¾ tsp. black pepper
½ tsp. garlic powder
Oil for frying
Hot Creamy Onion Sauce

Place tomato slices in shallow pan with buttermilk. Let stand 15 minutes. In shallow bowl, combine flour, cornmeal, salt, black pepper and garlic powder. Dredge tomato slices in cornmeal mixture. Deep fry in hot oil until golden brown. Drain on paper towels. Serve with Hot Creamy Onion Sauce

Hot Creamy Onion Sauce:

1 (15-oz.) can cream of onion soup
2 T. hot sauce
½ tsp. ground red pepper
2 T. sour cream
Milk, if needed

In small saucepan, whisk together soup, hot sauce, red pepper and sour cream. Heat on medium until hot. If sauce seems too thick, add milk until desired consistency. Keep hot until serving.

Note: Throughout the deep South you will find many versions of this Southern favorite. This one is especially good when served along side your Sunday afternoon fried chicken or those slow-basted barbecue pork ribs fresh off the grill.

Country Green Beans and Onions in Peanut Sauce

¼ c. chopped bacon
¼ c. onion, chopped
2 T. creamy peanut butter
½ c. light cream
½ tsp. salt
½ tsp. pepper
2 (15-oz.) cans cut green beans, drained
¼ c. chopped, roasted peanuts

In medium saucepan, sauté bacon and onion until tender. Stir in peanut butter. when peanut butter is melted, whisk in light cream, salt and pepper. When smooth, add green beans and heat on low heat until heated thoroughly. Sprinkle with chopped nuts when serving.

Note: An old Georgia favorite. Delicious when served with fried or baked chicken.

Cheesy Turnip Casserole

6 to 8 med. turnip roots, peeled and sliced ⅛ inch thick
2 med. onions, sliced thin
4 T. margarine
1 c. whipping cream
1½ c. grated white cheese
3 slices bacon, fried and crumbled
½ c. cracker crumbs
Margarine for dotting

In saucepan, boil turnip roots until tender crisp. Drain. In buttered casserole, layer ⅓ of turnips. Top with ⅓ of onions. Dot with ⅓ of margarine; drizzle with ⅓ of whipping cream. Sprinkle with ⅓ of the cheese. Next sprinkle with ⅓ of crumbled bacon. Repeat layers twice more. Sprinkle top of casserole with cracker crumbs and dot with margarine. Bake in preheated 350° oven for 30 to 35 minutes.

Note: Try serving this on a cold winter night. Make sure it's piping hot from the oven. The family will love it!

CREAMED TURNIP GREENS

⅓ c. chopped onion
⅓ c. chopped red bell pepper
2 cloves garlic, minced
2 (15-oz.) cans chopped turnip
   greens

1 T. vinegar
1½ tsp. sugar
¼ tsp. salt
½ tsp. black pepper
4 oz. cream cheese, softened

    Sauté onion and pepper together until soft. Add garlic and turnips. Let simmer 10 minutes. Stir in vinegar, sugar, salt and pepper. Then stir in cream cheese. Keep over low heat, stirring until cheese is melted in. Keep hot until serving.

    Note: A pleasant change from creamed spinach. Delicious with pork loin roast or country fried steak.

CREAMED TURNIP ROOTS AND ONIONS

4 med. turnip roots, peeled and
   sliced
¾ c. frozen pearl onions
1 T. butter

1 T. flour
¼ tsp. salt
¾ c. milk
¼ c. heavy cream

    Cook turnip roots in salted boiling water 15 to 20 minutes. During last 10 minutes, add pearl onions. When done, remove from heat and drain. In small saucepan, melt butter; blend in flour and salt. Add milk, whisking to prevent lumps. Stir constantly until thickened and bubbly. Stir in heavy cream. Pour over turnips and onions; toss lightly and turn into buttered casserole. Heat in 350° oven 20 minutes before serving.

    Note: This dish is delicious with pork or chicken. Try it with succulent breaded pork chops or crispy fried chicken for your next Sunday dinner.

SOUTHERN HOSPITALITY SUCCOTASH

1 (16-oz.) pkg. frozen green lima
   beans
¼ c. chopped onion
1 T. butter
1 (15 oz.) whole kernel corn,
   slightly drained

1 (2-oz.) jar diced pimiento,
   drained
3 strips bacon, fried crisp and
   crumbled

In large saucepan, combine beans, onion and butter and cook according to package directions. When done, add corn and pimiento. Heat to boiling. Remove from heat. Serve with sprinkling with crumbled bacon.

Note: For your next roast beef dinner, try this delicious side dish. It's simple and oh so good!

SOUTHERN CARROT FLUFF

16-oz. pkg. frozen baby carrots
2 T. margarine, softened
¼ c. brown sugar, packed
¼ tsp. grated nutmeg

½ tsp. salt
Marshmallow fluff
¼ c. chopped walnuts, toasted

Cook carrots according to package directions. Drain. Place in buttered casserole dish and toss with margarine, brown sugar, nutmeg and salt. Top with enough marshmallow fluff to cover entire top surface ¼ to ½ inch thick. Sprinkle with walnuts and bake in 350° oven for 15 to 20 minutes or until lightly browned.

Note: This is a nice change from sweet potatoes. Goes very well with pork or chicken and is attractive on a buffet.

Golden Eggplant Bake

¾ c. pancake mix
¾ c. water
¼ tsp. garlic powder
¼ tsp. ground red pepper
¼ tsp. black pepper
¼ tsp. salt
8 (½-inch) thick slices of eggplant

1½ c. panko crumbs
Oil for frying
12 slices bacon
1 sm. onion, thinly sliced
1½ c. grated cheddar or Pepper Jack cheese

In shallow pan combine pancake mix, water, garlic powder, red pepper, black pepper and salt. Blend until smooth. Dip eggplant slices in batter and dredge heavily in panko crumbs. In skillet fry slices in hot oil until golden brown and crisp. Remove and drain on paper towels and set aside. Discard oil and fry bacon in skillet until crisp. Drain and set aside. Remove bacon fat from skillet reserving 2 tablespoons to sauté onion in. When onion is transparent, remove from skillet and set aside. In 8-inch square baking dish, place 4 of the eggplant slices for bottom layer. Crumble half of the bacon over eggplant. Follow with half of the onions and sprinkle with half of the cheese. Layer remaining eggplant over cheese and repeat process. Bake at 375° in oven for 20 to 30 minutes.

Note: This makes an attractive main brunch dish. To complete the menu, serve with crisp lettuce wedges and a fresh fruit cup.

Deep South Cornmeal Fried Squash

2 lbs. yellow squash, sliced ¼ inch thick
1 c. buttermilk
1 c. yellow cornmeal
½ tsp. ground red pepper
¼ tsp. garlic powder

¼ tsp. onion powder
1 tsp. paprika
¼ tsp. black pepper
¼ tsp. salt
Oil for frying

Marinate squash slices in buttermilk for 20 minutes. Meanwhile, in shallow pan, combine cornmeal, red pepper, garlic powder, onion powder, paprika, black pepper and salt. Discard buttermilk and dredge each slice of squash in cornmeal mixture. Fry in hot oil until golden brown on each side. Drain on paper towels.

Note: For a meatless supper on a hot summer evening, serve this Old South favorite with mac 'n cheese, collard greens, sliced tomatoes and cornbread and top it all off with a slice of Southern Lemon Cream Cake or home-churned peach ice cream.

SOUTHERN FRIED SQUASH PATTIES

1 c. cooked yellow squash, drained and finely chopped
1 sm. onion, finely chopped and sautéed
½ tsp. salt
½ tsp. black pepper
¼ c. toasted chopped pecans
1 egg, beaten
½ c. flour (or less)
1 c. cornflake crumbs
Oil for frying

In mixing bowl, combine squash, onion, salt pepper and pecans. Mix well. Add egg and blend thoroughly. Gradually add flour until mixture will hold a shape when formed. Form into 1½-inch patties. Dredge in cornflake crumbs. Heat oil in large skillet and fry patties until golden brown on both sides. Drain on paper towels.

Note: For a vegetarian supper, serve these crisp patties with other Southern favorites such as okra and tomatoes, mac 'n cheese, corn on the cob and Southern sweet tea.

FARMER'S MAC 'N CHEESE CASSEROLE

2 c. elbow macaroni, cooked
1½ to 2 c. canned cheese sauce
2 T. mayonnaise
1 tsp. garlic powder
1 tsp. paprika
1 T. parsley flakes
3 T. chopped pimiento
½ c. grated cheddar cheese
½ c. grated mozzarella cheese
½ c. whole kernel corn
¾ c. broccoli flowerets, cooked

In large mixing bowl, combine cooked pasta and 1½ cups cheese sauce, mayonnaise, garlic powder, paprika, parsley flakes and pimiento. Mix well. Fold in cheddar and mozzarella cheese. When blended, fold in corn and broccoli. If needed, add additional cheese sauce. Turn into 1½-quart casserole. Bake at 350° for 30 to 45 minutes.

Note: Without a doubt this casserole stands alone; no need for meat. You can substitute whatever you have in your garden for the corn and broccoli, green beans, carrots, turnip roots to name just a few. Just serve with a salad and iced tea for a down home supper on the farm.

Riverboat Puppies

1¾ c. yellow cornmeal
½ c. flour
1 tsp. sugar
¾ tsp. baking soda
½ tsp. salt
½ c. diced onion

½ c. finely chopped okra
¾ c. buttermilk
¼ c. beer
1 egg
1 tsp. hot sauce
Oil for frying

In large bowl, mix together cornmeal, flour, sugar, baking soda and salt. Blend well. Add onion and okra. Stir until well blended. In separate bowl, combine buttermilk, beer and egg. Add to dry ingredients. Stir until all ingredients are combined. Drop by heaping teaspoon into hot oil. Fry until golden brown turning once during frying. Remove and drain on paper towels.

Note: Nothing takes the place of crispy fried hush puppies with fresh caught catfish. These pups have a special flavor from its secret ingredient.. .BEER!

Nutty Vidalia Onion Rings

1 c. pancake mix
1 c. water
¼ c. very finely chopped, roasted peanuts
½ tsp. paprika

¾ c. cracker crumbs
1 lg. Vidalia onion, sliced and separated into rings
Oil for frying

In small mixing bowl, whisk together pancake mix and water until smooth. Set aside. In shallow pan, combine peanuts, paprika and crumbs. Mix well. Dip each onion ring into pancake batter. Shake off excess batter then dredge in crumb mixture. Fry in hot oil until golden brown on both sides. Drain on paper towels.

Note: Your family and friends will go "nuts" over these sweet and nutty onion rings! Perfect with steaks or burgers off the grill or just by themselves.

DAD'S FAVORITE LIMA BEAN CASSEROLE

1 (16-oz.) pkg. frozen green lima beans
½ c. chopped onion
⅓ c. ketchup
⅓ c. tomato sauce
½ c. cracker crumbs
2 T. butter or margarine

Cook lima beans according to package directions adding onion during last 10 minutes of cooking time. When beans are tender, drain off liquid. Stir in ketchup and tomato sauce. Pour into buttered casserole dish. Top with cracker crumbs and dot with butter. Bake at 350° for 20 minutes or until crumbs are golden.

Note: This was Dad's favorite way to eat lima beans. Whenever we had any lima bean dish, the ketchup bottle had to be on the table.

DIXIE BAKED BEANS

¼ c. diced salt pork
¼ c. chopped onion
½ tsp. minced garlic
2 (15-oz.) cans pork 'n beans
⅓ c. brown sugar
1 T. prepared mustard
1 T. ketchup
Salt and pepper
¼ c. Kentucky bourbon
4 slices bacon

In small skillet, sauté salt pork 5 minutes. Add onion and sauté 5 minutes more. Add garlic and sauté 3 minutes longer. Remove from heat and set aside. In mixing bowl, combine pork 'n beans, brown sugar, mustard and ketchup. Season with salt and pepper. Add bourbon and blend well. Fold in onion mixture. Spoon into casserole. Place bacon slices on top and bake in 375° oven for 1 hour.

Note: Next time you fire up the grill, be sure to get out the old iron skillet for these Deep South beans. They are the perfect addition to any barbecue!

Golden Corn Nuggets

⅔ c. all-purpose flour
⅔ c. yellow cornmeal
⅔ c. quick grits
1½ tsp. baking powder
1 tsp. salt

¾ tsp. onion powder
¼ c. vegetable oil
½ c. water
Vegetable oil for frying

Blend flour, cornmeal, grits, baking powder, salt and onion powder together. Blend in oil and water until thoroughly mixed. Heat enough vegetable oil in skillet to be ½ inch deep. Drop nugget batter in by ¾ teaspoon and fry until golden brown.

Note: Mmm Mmm good! Great with fried fish or chicken or fry a batch to have with ice cold beer.

Sweet Potato-Marshmallow Crunch

6 lg. sweet potatoes, baked
¼ c. butter
¼ tsp. salt
1 c. miniature marshmallows
3 T. butter
⅔ c. flour

⅓ c. brown sugar
¼ tsp. salt
½ tsp. baking soda
⅓ c. chopped walnuts
⅓ c. rolled oats

Peel sweet potatoes and place in large mixing bowl. Mash until smooth. Add butter and salt. Blend well. Divide mixture putting half in casserole dish. Spread evenly. Top with single layer of marshmallows. Top with remaining potatoes. Spread evenly. Set aside. In mixing bowl, cut butter, flour and sugar together to resemble coarse crumbs. Mix in salt, baking soda, walnuts and oats. Do not over mix. Evenly sprinkle crumb mixture over potatoes. Press lightly. Bake in 350° oven for 35 minutes or until crumb is golden.

Note: Make a double batch for that family get-to-gether. Goes great with glazed ham and turnip greens!

Sweet Potato Turnovers

1 (17.3-oz.) pkg. frozen puff pastry sheets
1 c. baked and mashed sweet potatoes
½ tsp. salt
¼ tsp. cinnamon
1 c. miniature marshmallows
1 egg, lightly beaten
Sugar

On lightly floured work board, roll thawed pastry sheets to ⅛-inch thickness. Cut 6-inch rounds; sheets should yield 6 to 8 rounds. Set aside. Combine mashed sweet potatoes, salt and cinnamon. Divide between pastry rounds. Divide marshmallows between pastries lightly pressing into sweet potato filling. Fold pastry circles in half and crimp edges well with fork. Transfer onto baking sheet lined with parchment paper. Brush each pastry with beaten egg and sprinkle with sugar. Bake in 350° oven that is preheated for 20 to 30 minutes or until golden brown.

Note: Makes a great side with a baked ham dinner or doubles as a tasty dessert treat with hot coffee or tea.

Country Buttermilk Bacon Whipped Potatoes

4 lg. potatoes, peeled and cubed
⅓ to ½ c. buttermilk
2 T. margarine
¾ tsp. salt
3 slices bacon, fried crisp and crumbled
1 tsp. dried parsley flakes

In 2-quart saucepan, boil potatoes until tender. Drain. Mash until smooth. Beat in buttermilk, margarine and salt. Use as much buttermilk as needed to make potatoes a fluffy consistency. Fold in crumbled bacon. Sprinkle with parsley flakes before serving.

Note: A perfect side to Country Fried Steak. Add a platter of sliced tomatoes, buttermilk biscuits and a blackberry cobbler and you've got a true Southern supper.

TWICE BAKED SWEET POTATO BOATS

4 med. red sweet potatoes, washed, dried and rubbed with oil
½ c. sour cream
2 T. butter or margarine
¼ c. chopped chives
2 slices bacon, fried crisp and crumbled

Place sweet potatoes on baking sheet and bake 1 hour in 425° oven. Remove from oven; cut slit in top of potatoes. Scoop out potato leaving a ¼-inch wall. Combine potatoes, sour cream and butter or margarine in mixing bowl. Mash until fluffy. Fold in chives and bacon. Fill potato shells with potato mixture. Return to 425° oven for 20 to 30 minutes.

Note: A new twist on an old favorite. Try them with grilled meats, smoked sausages or as a main dish for brunch with a salad.

CHEESE STUFFED FRIED POTATO PUFFS

1½ c. cold mashed potatoes
½ tsp. salt
½ tsp. baking powder
1 T. flour
1 egg
8 (1-inch) cubes cheddar cheese
1 egg beaten with 1 tsp. water
1 c. panko crumbs
Oil for deep frying

In medium mixing bowl, beat potatoes, salt, baking powder, flour and egg for 2 minutes on medium speed with electric hand mixer or until well blended. Divide potato mixture into 8 equal portions. Form mixture around cubes of cheese to form a ball. Dip each ball into beaten egg and then dredge in panko crumbs. Refrigerate for ½ hour. Heat enough oil in heavy pot to be 1½ inches deep. Remove balls from refrigerator. Carefully add balls into hot oil. Fry until golden brown turning as needed to brown evenly. Drain on paper towels.

Note: Excellent surrounding a beef roast or baked corned beef. Any cheese can be used. For an exceptional treat with corned beef, try Havarti cheese with dill.

MAGGIE'S CHICK-A-DEE POTATOES

8 med. potatoes, peeled and cubed
½ c. chopped onion
½ c. canned cream of chicken soup
¼ c. milk
¾ c. grated Pepper Jack cheese
½ c. cracker crumbs
2 T. butter
Salt and pepper to taste

In 2-quart saucepan, boil potatoes and onions together. When done, drain well and mash. Add cream of chicken soup and milk. Beat until fluffy. Place in a buttered casserole dish and top with cheese and cracker crumbs. Dot with butter and sprinkle with salt and pepper. Bake at 350° for 20 to 30 minutes or until bubbly and brown.

Note: This chicken laced casserole is down home "comfort food." We named it after Maggie, our best laying hen.

UNCLE ROY'S FRIED POTATOES

Oil for frying
4 lg. potatoes, peeled and sliced ⅛ inch thick
2 med. onions, peeled and thinly sliced
4 T. flour
1½ c. chicken broth
Salt
Black pepper
2 tsp. hot pepper sauce

Heat oil in heavy skillet. Add potatoes and onions and fry until soft and tender and beginning to brown. Remove from skillet and keep warm in ovenproof dish at 350° while making gravy. Drain off oil reserving 4 tablespoons in skillet. Add flour and cook stirring constantly until golden brown roux. Roux should be dark in color. Add broth and whisk until smooth. Add salt and pepper to taste. Add hot pepper sauce. Cook until gravy is thick and rich. Pour over potatoes and serve.

Note: Our Uncle Roy came up with this lip-smackin' recipe while staying in an old cabin one winter. They are fantastic with fried salt pork (or as we say down South, "fat back").

TYBEE ISLAND STUFFED POTATOES

4 lg. baking potatoes
3 T. margarine
4 oz. cream cheese, softened
¼ c. sour cream
1 c. chopped, cooked shrimp
1 tsp. finely minced garlic
4 oz. shredded Havarti cheese with dill
1 tsp. dried parsley
Butter
Paprika

Bake potatoes in 400° oven for 1 hour. Remove from oven and trim ¼ inch off top. Carefully scoop out flesh leaving ¼-inch wall and bottom. In mixing bowl, mash potatoes with margarine until smooth. Beat in cream cheese and sour cream. Fold in shrimp, garlic, cheese and parsley. Spoon mixture back into potato shells, dot with butter and sprinkle with paprika. Bake at 400° for 20 to 30 minutes.

Note: This recipe can turn an ordinary steak dinner into an elegant turf 'n surf. It's also great with any seafood dinner and makes an excellent brunch when served with a salad and a cup of soup.

JEWELED SWEET POTATO BAKE

4 lg. baked sweet potatoes, peeled
2 T. margarine
⅔ c. whole cranberry sauce
1 c. miniature marshmallows
⅓ c. chopped walnuts

In mixing bowl, mash sweet potatoes with margarine until smooth. Fold in cranberry sauce. Place mixture in buttered casserole. Top with marshmallows and walnuts. Bake in 350° oven for 15 to 20 minutes or until marshmallows are golden and puffy.

Note: Next time you want to spruce up your turkey dinner, this is the perfect answer. They are great served with a juicy baked ham too.

SAPELO TOMATO GRITS

2 c. tomato juice
2 c. half-and-half
1 c. quick grits
1 tsp. salt
2 tsp. hot red pepper sauce
½ tsp. garlic powder
⅓ c. flaked crab meat

In 1½-quart saucepan, heat tomato juice and half-and-half. Slowly stir in grits, salt, pepper sauce and garlic powder. Reduce heat to medium-low. Cover. Cook 5 minutes or until thickened, stirring occasionally. Remove from heat and serve immediately.

Note: Delicious served with fried catfish and creamy coleslaw.

Beer Battered Fried Okra

½ c. pancake mix
⅓ c. beer
⅛ c. water
¼ tsp. cayenne pepper
½ c. yellow cornmeal

¼ c. flour
½ tsp. salt
2 c. sliced okra
Oil for frying

In mixing bowl, combine pancake mix, beer, water and cayenne pepper. Set aside. In shallow pan, combine cornmeal and flour. Toss together and add salt. When well blended, add a few pieces of okra at a time coating well. When all pieces have been coated, heat oil in heavy skillet (½ inch deep) and fry okra in single layer not over crowding until golden brown. Add more oil as needed. Repeat until all okra is fried. Drain on heavy paper towels. Serve hot.

Note: This recipe can be used in so many ways! Excellent as a side to fried chicken, fish or pork. But is a great cocktail food with drinks and also as croutons in a creamy chowder.

Peppered Greens

¼ c. diced salt pork
1 sm. onion, chopped
¼ c. chopped, roasted red pepper
2 (15-oz.) cans greens, collards, turnips or mustard greens

2 T. vinegar
1 tsp. sugar
1 tsp. oil
Salt and pepper to taste

Sauté salt pork in heavy saucepan for 5 minutes. Add onion and cook until tender. Add red pepper and greens. Stir in vinegar, sugar and oil. Season with salt and pepper. Heat 10 to 15 minutes or until thoroughly heated. If too tart, add a little extra sugar.

Note: This is a quick, healthy dish when made with canned or frozen greens but if you're fortunate enough to have a nice kitchen garden use some freshly picked greens. Prepare your greens to your liking then add the rest of the ingredients listed. And be sure to serve them with good ol' Southern fried chicken!

Creamy Tomato Grits

2 c. milk
2 c. tomato juice
½ tsp. garlic powder
¾ tsp. salt

1½ tsp. hot sauce
¾ c. quick grits
1 T. butter

In saucepan, combine milk, tomato juice, garlic powder, salt and hot sauce. Heat until hot but not boiling. Stir in grits; cook 5 minutes, stirring often. Remove from heat, add butter and stir. Cover tightly and let stand 3 to 5 minutes before serving.

Note: These spicy, creamy grits will steal the show at your next fish fry. They're terrific used in shrimp 'n grits and add a nice kick to any Southern morning breakfast.

Baked Potato Casserole

4 lg. baking potatoes
¾ c. sour cream
¼ c. heavy whipping cream
3 T. margarine, softened
8 slices bacon, fried crisp and crumbled

½ c. chopped green onions
1½ c. shredded cheddar cheese
Salt and pepper

In 400° oven, bake potatoes for 1 hour. Cool slightly. Peel and slice ¼ inch thick. In medium buttered casserole, place single layer of potatoes. In small mixing bowl, combine sour cream, whipping cream and margarine. Blend well. Spread ½ of sour cream mixture over potato layer. Sprinkle with ½ of bacon, onions and cheese. Season with salt and pepper. Dot with ½ of margarine. Repeat layer of potatoes, sour cream mixture, bacon, onions and cheese. Dot with remaining butter. Bake in preheated 375° oven for 30 minutes or until bubbly and beginning to brown.

Note: This is a very versatile dish, it can accompany just about any meat or seafood and is great for patio parties, barbecues, or just a nice dish to bring to a potluck.

CREAMED ONIONS AND GREEN BEANS

1 (14½-oz.) can chicken broth
1 (12-oz.) bag frozen cut green beans
⅔ c. frozen pearl onions
¼ c. heavy whipping cream
¾ tsp. salt

Substituting chicken broth for water, cook green beans and pearl onion together according to package directions. Cook until tender. Drain broth off reserving ¼ cup. Combine reserved broth with whipping cream. Return to beans and onions and beat thoroughly before serving.

Note: A favorite of Grandma's She always served them with Southern fried chicken. Delicious!!

POTATO CHEESE BAKE

6 med. potatoes, peeled and sliced thin
1 lg. onion, finely chopped
½ c. chopped red bell pepper
2 cloves garlic, crushed
Salt and pepper
Butter
1 (10¾-oz.) can cheddar cheese soup
1 c. heavy cream
½ c. cracker crumbs
2 T. butter

Butter 1½-quart casserole. Arrange ⅓ of potatoes in single layer in bottom of casserole. Sprinkle half of onions and red pepper over potatoes. Sprinkle with half of garlic. Season to taste with salt and pepper. Dot with butter. Combine soup with heavy cream until well blended and drizzle potato layer with ⅓ of soup mixture. Repeat process ending with ⅓ of potatoes on top. Pour remaining soup mixture over top. Sprinkle with cracker crumbs. Dot with butter. Cover with foil and bake in 350° oven for 1 hour. Remove foil and bake 15 minutes longer or until brown and potatoes test done.

Note: This tantalizing side enhances any entree and can double as a main course by adding diced ham or chicken in the layers.

Recipe Favorites

Helpful Hints

- Certain meats, like ribs and pot roast, can be parboiled before grilling to reduce the fat content.

- Pound meat lightly with a mallet or rolling pin, pierce with a fork, sprinkle lightly with meat tenderizer, and add marinade. Refrigerate for 20 minutes and cook or grill for a quick and succulent meat.

- Marinating is a cinch if you use a plastic bag. The meat stays in the marinade and it's easy to turn. Cleanup is easy; just toss the bag.

- It's easier to thinly slice meat if it's partially frozen.

- Adding tomatoes to roasts naturally tenderizes the meat as tomatoes contain an acid that works well to break down meats.

- Whenever possible, cut meat across the grain; this will make it easier to eat and also give it a more attractive appearance.

- When frying meat, sprinkle paprika on the meat to turn it golden brown.

- Thaw all meats in the refrigerator for maximum safety.

- Refrigerate poultry promptly after purchasing. Keep it in the coldest part of your refrigerator for up to 2 days. Freeze poultry for longer storage. Never leave poultry at room temperature for over 2 hours.

- When frying chicken, canola oil provides a milder taste, and it contains healthier amounts of saturated and polyunsaturated fats. Do not cover the chicken once it has finished cooking because covering will cause the coating to lose its crispness.

- One pound of boneless chicken equals approximately 3 cups of cubed chicken.

- Generally, red meats should reach 160° and poultry should reach 180° before serving. If preparing fish, the surface of the fish should flake off with a fork.

- Rub lemon juice on fish before cooking to enhance the flavor and help maintain a good color.

- Scaling a fish is easier if vinegar is rubbed on the scales first.

- When grilling fish, the rule of thumb is to cook 5 minutes on each side per inch of thickness. For example, cook a 2-inch thick fillet for 10 minutes per side. Before grilling, rub with oil to seal in moisture.

Main Dishes

SUMMERTIME LEMON FRIED CHICKEN

1 (3-lb.) fryer, cut up, washed and drained	1 c. flour
Juice of 1 sm. lemon	1 tsp. salt
½ tsp. grated lemon zest	1 tsp. lemon pepper
1½ c. buttermilk	Oil for frying
	Thin sliced lemon for garnish

Place chicken in large mixing bowl. Combine lemon juice, lemon zest and buttermilk. Pour over chicken and let marinate for 2 hours or overnight in refrigerator. When ready to fry, drain chicken; discard marinade. In shallow pan, combine flour, salt and lemon pepper. Heavily dredge chicken in flour. Heat oil in heavy skillet and fry until golden brown, turning once. When done, remove from oil and drain on paper towels. Place on platter and garnish with lemon slices.

Note: Get down the picnic basket and head for the lake!

EASY SOUTHERN FRIED CHICKEN 'N PUFFS

1 chicken, cut up
1 c. all-purpose flour
1½ tsp. salt
1 tsp. black pepper
Oil for frying
1 (10-oz.) can biscuits

2 T. butter
2 T. flour
¼ tsp. salt
½ tsp. black pepper
1 to 1½ c. milk

Wash and lightly dry chicken pieces. Combine flour, salt and pepper in shallow pan. Add chicken 1 or 2 pieces at a time tossing and turning to coat evenly. Drop in hot oil and fry until golden brown. Drain on paper towels. When all chicken has been fried, drop biscuits into hot oil being careful not to over crowd. Fry until puffed and brown turning once. Drain on paper towels. In separate small skillet, melt butter. Whisk in flour, salt, pepper and milk until smooth and no lumps remain. Cook over medium heat until thick and bubbly. Serve along side chicken and puffs.

Note: This is a Deep South favorite. Have a platter of sliced home grown tomatoes and a pot of peppered greens and you'll have all you need for a down home supper. Don't forget the blackberry cobbler and home-churned '"nilla" ice cream.

"HOT" FRIED CHICKEN

1 c. flour
¾ tsp. salt
¾ tsp. ground red pepper

¼ tsp. black pepper
3-lb. fryer, cut up
Oil for frying

Combine flour, salt, red pepper and black pepper together. Heavily dredge chicken pieces in flour mixture. Heat oil in large skillet. Drop chicken in and fry until golden brown, turning only once.

Note: Serve with yellow rice and tomato gravy. You can add crispy fried okra too!

SPICY BUTTERMILK CHICKEN LIVERS WITH CREAMY GRAVY

½ c. buttermilk
⅛ c. red hot sauce
1 lb. chicken livers, rinsed and dried
1 c. flour plus 2 T.
½ tsp. salt
½ tsp. black pepper
Oil for frying
½ c. heavy cream
½ to ¾ c. milk
¼ c. canned French-fried onions

In medium mixing bowl, combine buttermilk and hot sauce. Add chicken livers and let set for 1 to 2 hours in refrigerator. In separate shallow pan, combine flour, salt and pepper. Remove chicken livers from buttermilk and dredge heavily in flour mixture. Heat ½ inch deep oil in heavy skillet. Add chicken livers and fry until golden brown. Remove from oil and drain. Pour off all but 2 tablespoons of oil. To oil in skillet, add 2 tablespoons of flour whisking until smooth. Whisk in cream and milk. Cook until thickened and stir in French-fried onions.

Note: Serve these delightfully spicy chicken livers over hot biscuits fresh out of the oven and plenty of red hot sauce.

SUNDAY NIGHT CHICKEN 'N RICE CASSEROLE

½ c. chopped celery
½ c. chopped onion
2 c. cubed, cooked chicken
½ c. diced, cooked carrots
1 (10¾-oz.) can cream of chicken soup
1¼ c. milk
1 tsp. salt
1 tsp. black pepper
4 c. cooked white rice
½ c. finely crushed saltines
3 T. margarine

In saucepan, sauté celery and onion in butter until soft. Add chicken and carrots and sauté 5 minutes longer. Remove from heat. In mixing bowl, whisk together soup and milk until smooth. Stir into chicken mixture along with salt and pepper. Gently fold in rice and turn into 2-quart casserole. Top with crushed saltines and dot with margarine. Bake in preheated oven at 350° for 20 to 30 minutes or until topping is golden and casserole is hot.

Note: For an easy no-fuss Sunday dinner, serve with creamy coleslaw, sliced fresh tomatoes, hard rolls and butter and, of course, iced tea.

Blackberry Glazed Chicken Breasts

1 (8-oz.) pkg. cream cheese
½ tsp. minced garlic
¼ c. chopped, toasted pecans
4 boneless chicken breasts
Salt and pepper

4 T. butter
½ c. seedless blackberry jam
¼ c. blackberry wine
½ tsp. cornstarch

In medium mixing bowl, blend together cream cheese and garlic until smooth. Stir in pecans and set aside. On work surface, pound chicken breasts to ½-inch thickness. Salt and pepper. Divide cheese mixture into 4 equal portions. Place a portion in center of each breast. Roll up and secure with toothpick. In buttered baking dish, place breasts seam side down and top each breast with 1 tablespoon of butter. In separate bowl, combine jam and wine and blend in cornstarch. In 425° oven, bake chicken covered for 30 minutes. Remove cover and begin basting heavily with blackberry mixture and continue baking 30 to 45 minutes longer or until well glazed.

Note: Blackberries grow wild along the rivers in western Georgia. During the Depression my Grandpa made blackberry wine in the attic. It's the wine in this dish that gives it that special touch. Be sure your side dishes are a little tart so that the sweetness of the blackberries stand out.

Country Chicken Bake

2 lbs. chicken thighs, salted and peppered
2 T. oil
1½ c. canned, stewed tomatoes
1 (8-oz.) can tomato sauce
¼ c. red wine
1 clove garlic, minced

1 tsp. celery flakes
1½ T. sugar
½ tsp. salt
1 lg. onion, sliced
½ c. chopped green pepper
½ c. chicken broth

Brown chicken in oil in ovenproof Dutch oven. In separate bowl, combine stewed tomatoes, tomato sauce, wine, garlic, celery flakes, sugar and salt. Blend well. Layer onion slices and green pepper over chicken and cover with tomato mixture. Cover and bake at 375° for 1 to 1½ hours adding chicken broth as needed.

Note: Serve with hot, fluffy rice and you've got a quick and easy version of Country Captain.

LOW COUNTRY STUFFED PEPPERS

4 med. red bell peppers
1½ c. diced, cooked white meat of chicken
1½ c. cooked yellow rice
1 egg, beaten
3 T. vegetable oil
1 sm. onion, chopped
3 T. flour
1½ c. chicken broth
1 c. canned stewed tomatoes, drained
½ c. sliced, cooked okra
1 tsp. salt
1 tsp. black pepper

Cut bell peppers in half lengthwise. Remove seeds. Place in lightly greased baking dish cut side up and roast in 400° oven for 10 minutes. Meanwhile in mixing bowl, combine chicken, rice and egg. Set aside. In large skillet, heat oil and add onion and flour and brown until a dark golden roux. Add chicken broth gradually, stirring constantly to avoid lumping. When smooth and beginning to thicken, add tomatoes and okra. Stir together and add salt and pepper. Set aside. Divide rice mixture between pepper halves, packing them full. Pour gravy over peppers and cover. Return to 400° oven for 45 minutes.

Note: Crusty garlic bread and creamy coleslaw make this a complete low country meal.

RED PEPPER STUFFED CHICKEN

1 red bell pepper, chopped
1 sm. onion, chopped
1 sm. clove garlic, chopped
1 c. cracker crumbs
1 egg, beaten
4 lg. boneless chicken breasts, flattened
4 T. butter, softened
Kosher salt

Sauté bell pepper, onion and garlic in a little oil until soft. Blend pepper mixture with cracker crumbs and egg until completely blended. With skin side down, place ¼ of pepper stuffing on center of each chicken breast. Roll jellyroll-fashion and secure with toothpick. Place seam side down in glass baking dish. Butter sides and top of each breast with softened butter and sprinkle with Kosher salt. Cover and bake in 400° oven for 1 hour or until tests done.

Note: A perfect side for this spicy dish is rice pilaf or for a more exotic twist try couscous!

Shrimp Creole Stuffed Cornish Hens

4 Cornish hens, prepared to stuff
2 c. cooked rice
¼ c. chopped onion
¼ c. chopped bell pepper
¼ c. chopped celery
1 clove garlic, minced
½ c. cooked, chopped shrimp
½ c. diced stewed tomatoes, drained
¼ tsp. seasoned salt
¼ tsp. cayenne pepper
Softened butter
Paprika

Place well drained Cornish hens on lightly greased baking pan. Set aside. In mixing bowl, combine rice, onion, bell pepper, celery, garlic, shrimp, tomatoes, salt and cayenne. Blend well. Divide mixture between Cornish hens and stuff. Heavily butter outside of hens and sprinkle with paprika. Bake in preheated 400° oven for 1 hour or until done.

Note: A very elegant dinner entree. Serve with fried okra and peppered greens for a delicious combination. For dessert be sure to serve River Road Bread Pudding with Bourbon Sauce.

SAVANNAH STYLE STUFFED CHICKEN BREASTS

1 (8-oz.) box dirty rice mix
½ c. chopped pecans, toasted
¼ c. finely chopped onion
1 egg, beaten
1 tsp. salt
1 tsp. pepper

4 boneless chicken breast
4 pats butter
1 (15-oz.) can whole cranberry sauce
¼ c. brown sugar
½ c. pink champagne

Prepare dirty rice mix according to package directions. When cooked and cooled, mix in chopped pecans, onion and egg. Divide rice mixture in half. Set half aside and divide remaining half into 4 equal portions. Salt and pepper the chicken breasts. On work surface, pound chicken breasts to ½ inch thick. Place 1 portion of rice in center of each breast. Roll up and secure with toothpick. In large buttered casserole, line bottom with remaining rice. Place breasts seam side down on top of rice. Place a pat of butter on each chicken breast. Preheat oven to 400°. Bake for 30 minutes covered. While chicken is baking, in medium mixing bowl, combine cranberry sauce, brown sugar and champagne together. After chicken has baked for 30 minutes, begin basting frequently with cranberry mixture and continue baking uncovered for 45 minutes longer.

Note: For a truly Southern plantation dinner, this elegant dish needs only 2 delicate vegetable sides such as braised Brussels sprouts or buttered baby carrots and, of course, a traditional pecan pie and whipped cream for dessert!

CHEESY SHRIMP 'N GRITS

¼ c. chopped celery
¼ c. chopped onion
¼ c. chopped green pepper
1 c. water
1 c. milk
1 (10¾-oz.) can cream of shrimp soup

¾ c. quick grits
½ tsp. garlic powder
½ c. shredded Jack cheese
6 oz. sm. salad shrimp, cooked

Sauté celery, onion and green pepper in oil until tender. Set aside. In medium saucepan, whisk together water, milk and soup over high heat. Stir in grits and garlic powder and let cook 3 minutes. Add celery-onion mixture and cook 2 minutes longer. Remove from heat; stir in cheese and shrimp. Spoon into buttered casserole or individual ramekins and bake 20 minutes at 350°.

Note: This is an all-time favorite throughout the South. No matter where you live you'll love it too!

Golden Tender Fried Shrimp

½ c. sour cream
½ c. milk
4 T. flour (or enough to make thick batter)
½ tsp. garlic powder

1 lb. med. shrimp, peeled, deveined and butterflied
1½ c. panko crumbs
Oil for frying

Combine sour cream, milk, flour and garlic powder. Beat until smooth. Dip shrimp in batter, shaking off excess before heavily dredging in crumbs. Fry in hot oil until golden and drain on paper towels.

Note: The batter for these shrimp is delectably light. They fry up golden brown and are absolutely scrumptious.

Uncle Nick's Stuffed Trout

1 clove garlic, minced
½ lb. cooked salad shrimp
1 c. cracker crumbs
3 T. butter, melted

4 lg. trout, cleaned
Salt and pepper
4 T. butter, melted

Combine garlic, shrimp and cracker crumbs together in mixing bowl. Add 3 tablespoons melted butter. Toss until well blended. Set aside. Sprinkle trout inside and out with salt and pepper. Divide shrimp mixture into 4 equal portions. Stuff each trout with a portion of mixture. Place trout in well greased shallow baking pan. Brush with melted butter. Cover pan with foil and bake in 400° preheated oven for 15 to 20 minutes or until fish flakes easily with a fork.

Note: This was Uncle Nick's own recipe. He was quite a fisherman and an excellent cook. It's a family favorite.

MOON RIVER FRIED FISH FILLETS

1 egg, beaten
½ c. buttermilk
1 T. hot sauce
¼ tsp. salt
½ c. cornmeal
½ c. fine cornflake crumbs
4 catfish fillets

Oil for frying
1 bell pepper, sliced
1 med. onion, sliced
3 T. oil
3 T. flour
¾ c. canned okra and tomatoes
  (undrained)

In shallow pan, combine egg, buttermilk, hot sauce and salt. Blend and set aside. In shallow pan, combine cornmeal and cornflake crumbs. Dip each fillet in buttermilk mixture then dredge in cornmeal mixture. Fry in hot oil until golden brown on both sides. Remove and drain on paper towels and keep warm in oven. In same skillet, sauté bell pepper and onion until tender. Remove and set aside. In separate skillet, heat 3 tablespoons of oil and blend in flour, cooking over medium heat to a dark golden roux. Stir in tomatoes and okra along with peppers and onions stirring all the while to prevent lumps. Add enough water, whisking while adding to create a medium thick gravy. Season with salt and pepper to taste and serve over fish fillets.

Note: This is a family favorite when we have a get-together at the boat house on the river.

NUT CRUSTED DEEP FRIED CATFISH

1½ lbs. catfish fillets
1 c. buttermilk
1 clove garlic, minced
2 T. hot sauce
1 c. flour

1 c. yellow cornmeal
½ c. finely chopped pecans
½ tsp. salt
Oil for frying

Marinate catfish in mixture of buttermilk, garlic and hot sauce for 1 hour in refrigerator. In mixing bowl, combine flour, cornmeal, nuts and salt. Remove catfish and discard buttermilk. Dredge in flour mixture and fry in hot oil until golden brown. Drain.

Note: If you're looking for something to please family and friends you can't go wrong with this recipe! It's versatile because it can be served with creamy slaw, Creole tartar sauce and hush puppies for a simple summer supper or pair it off with a rice pilaf and Caesar salad for an elegant dinner party.

RIVER ROAD FRIED FISH FILLETS

1 egg, beaten
½ c. buttermilk
Juice of ½ lemon
1½ lbs. fresh fish fillets (catfish, founder, etc.)

1 c. yellow cornmeal
½ tsp. salt
¾ tsp. ground red pepper
Oil for frying

Combine egg, buttermilk and lemon juice. Place fish fillets in buttermilk mixture and marinate ½ an hour. Meanwhile, combine cornmeal, salt and red pepper in shallow baking dish. Remove fillets from marinade; discard buttermilk mixture. Dredge fillets in cornmeal mixture and fry in hot oil until golden brown, about 2 to 3 minutes per side.

Note: Perfect recipe to use at an old-fashioned fish fry. Be sure to fry up plenty and have creamy coleslaw and hush puppies on hand. And don't forget the sweet tea.

HOT 'N CRISPY FISH FILLETS

1 c. tomato juice
2 T. hot sauce
Salt and pepper to taste
1½ lbs. catfish fillets
2 eggs, beaten

1 c. cornflake crumbs
1 c. yellow cornmeal
¼ c. chopped chives
Oil for frying

Combine tomato juice, hot sauce and salt and pepper in glass bowl. Place fish fillets in tomato juice mixture and let marinate for 1 or more hours in refrigerator. Beat eggs and set aside. Combine cornflake crumbs and cornmeal in shallow baking dish. When ready to cook, remove fillets; discard marinade. Dip each fillet in beaten egg and dredge in crumb mixture. Lower in hot oil. Fry until golden brown on both sides.

Note: Makes a great Sunday supper for the family or triple the recipe and have an old-fashion fish fry with friends and neighbors. Don't forget the hush puppies!

CORNBREAD STUFFED CATFISH

3 c. day-old cornbread crumbs
½ c. chopped onion, sautéed
4 slices bacon, fried crisp and crumbled
1 egg, beaten
1 T. hot sauce
½ c. buttermilk
½ tsp. salt
¾ tsp. black pepper
6 med. catfish fillets
1 egg, beaten
1 c. cornflake crumbs
6 pats butter
6 thin lemon slices

In medium mixing bowl, combine cornbread crumbs, onion, bacon, egg, hot sauce, buttermilk, salt and black pepper. Divide cornbread mixture into 6 equal portions. Place 1 portion on each catfish fillet. Roll and secure with toothpick. Place seam side down in buttered casserole. Brush top and sides with beaten egg. Pat on cornflake crumbs covering as much surface of each fillet as possible. Place 1 pat of butter on each fillet. Bake in preheated 350° oven for 30 minutes or until golden brown. Garnish each fillet with a lemon slice before serving.

Note: Don't know what to do with that leftover cornbread or corn muffins? Here's a way to turn it into a real treat for the family.

FRIED SALMON FINGERS

1½ lbs. salmon fillets, cut in 1-inch strips
1 c. buttermilk
1 c. pancake mix
1 c. water
½ tsp. garlic powder
1½ c. cornflake crumbs
Oil for frying

Place salmon in glass bowl with buttermilk and let marinate for 1 hour in refrigerator. In small mixing bowl, blend pancake mix with water and garlic powder. Remove salmon and discard buttermilk. Dip salmon fingers in batter mixture and dredge in cornflake crumbs. Lower into hot oil, fry until golden brown and drain.

Note: Savannah's English heritage shines through in these crunchy fingers. Serve them the traditional British way with "chips" and a delicate tartar sauce.

Cape Fear Oyster Pies

2 T. butter
½ c. chopped celery
½ c. chopped onion
½ c. cubed, cooked potatoes
½ tsp. salt
4 T. flour

1 c. heavy cream
¼ c. milk
½ tsp. ground red pepper
2 pt. oysters, rinsed and drained
1 sheet frozen puff pastry dough
1 egg, beaten

In saucepan, melt butter and sauté celery and onion until tender. Add potatoes and salt and remove from heat. In mixing bowl, whisk flour into cream and milk until smooth. Stir in red pepper. Stir into vegetable mixture, return to heat and continue stirring until thickened. Remove from heat and set aside. In 4 (8-ounce) ramekins, divide oysters equally. Spoon vegetable/cream mixture over oysters. Set aside. On floured surface, roll pastry dough to ⅛-inch thickness and cut 4 (6-inch) rounds. Place rounds on top of each ramekin crimping to seal edges. Brush with beaten egg. Place ramekins on baking sheet and bake in preheated 350° oven 20 to 30 minutes or until crust is golden brown.

Note: Oyster lovers will love this creamy, delicate dish!

Tybee Island Baked Eggs and Oysters

4 lg. fresh oysters, shucked
4 lg. eggs
1 tsp. salt
2 tsp. red hot pepper sauce

1 c. heavy cream
4 tsp. butter
½ c. grated fresh Parmesan cheese
2 tsp. dried parsley flakes

Preheat oven to 325°. In 4 individual, buttered (8-ounce) ramekins, place 1 oyster and top with 1 egg. Sprinkle with ¼ teaspoon salt, ½ teaspoon hot pepper sauce. Gently pour ¼ cup heavy cream over egg. Place 1 tablespoon butter on top. Sprinkle with ⅛ cup Parmesan, grated. Top with parsley flakes and bake for 20 minutes or until set.

Note: The sound of the surf and the ocean breeze sets the stage for this simple yet elegant light supper. Serve with Caesar salad, hard rolls and butter and tomato juice cocktail.

LOW COUNTRY SEAFOOD LASAGNA

¼ c. chopped green pepper
¼ c. chopped celery
2 cloves garlic, minced
¼ c. chopped onion
4 oz. bulk andouille sausage
28-oz. jar spaghetti sauce
¾ c. salad shrimp
4 oz. lump crabmeat

8-oz. pkg. farmers cheese
½ c. Parmesan cheese
1 egg, beaten
¾ tsp. garlic powder
¼ tsp. cayenne pepper
½ (12-oz.) pkg. no-baked lasagna
6 oz. grated mozzarella

Sauté green pepper, celery, garlic, onion and sausage until tender and done. Add spaghetti sauce and let simmer for ½ hour. Add shrimp and crab. Blend and remove from heat. In medium mixing bowl, break up farmers cheese. Mix in Parmesan cheese and beaten egg. Blend in garlic powder and cayenne pepper. Set aside. In 13 x 9-inch baking dish, spoon in enough sauce to cover bottom of dish. Layer lasagna sheets in single layer to cover bottom. Cover with ½ of the sauce. Layer another layer of lasagna sheets and cover with ½ of the cheese mixture. Sprinkle ½ of the mozzarella over cheese mixture. Repeat the layers ending with cheese. Cover with foil, crimping edges tight and bake 1 hour in preheated 400° oven or until tests done.

Note: Add a Caesar salad and crusty hot bread to make this a perfect Saturday night supper for family and friends.

BRANDIED PORK LOIN CHOPS WITH APPLES AND ONIONS

4 pork loin chops, ½ inch thick
1 lg. onion, thinly sliced
2 Granny Smith apples, peeled and sliced

2 cloves garlic, minced
Salt and pepper
½ c. apple cider
2 T. apple brandy

In greased baking dish, arrange pork chops with onions and apples layered on top. Sprinkle garlic over apples and follow with a sprinkling of salt and pepper. Combine cider and brandy and pour over entire mixture. Cover and bake at 425° for 1 hour. Remove cover and continue baking 15 minutes longer or until beginning to lightly brown.

Note: Pair off with buttermilk mashed potatoes and balsamic glazed Brussels sprouts for a meal sure to please the heartiest of appetites.

APPLE CHEESE PORK CUTLETS

1 lb. ground pork
½ lb. ground sausage
1 clove garlic, minced
1 egg, slightly beaten
½ tsp. salt
¾ tsp. black pepper

4 oz. softened cream cheese
½ c. apple pie filling, chopped
¾ c. fine cracker crumbs
Oil for frying
Apple cider gravy

Thoroughly combine pork, sausage, garlic, egg, salt and black pepper. Divide into 8 equal portions and form each portion into a ¼-inch thick patty. In a separate mixing bowl, combine apple filling and cream cheese and divide into 4 portions, placing 1 portion in center of 4 of the pork patties. Flatten apple filling so that it doesn't stand too high. Place remaining 4 patties on top of filled patties. Crimp edges firmly. Dredge in cracker crumbs and sauté in hot oil in large skillet until golden brown and tests done. Serve with apple cider gravy.

Apple Cider Gravy:

½ c. apple cider
1½ c. chicken broth
½ tsp. salt

½ tsp. pepper
2 T. cornstarch
¼ c. water

Combine cider and chicken broth in small saucepan. Add salt and pepper, stir and set aside. In small bowl stir cornstarch into water. Mix until smooth. Blend into broth mixture. Cook over medium heat to boiling. Boil for 1 minute, stirring constantly until thickened. Remove from heat and serve.

Note: Buttermilk whipped potatoes are the perfect compliment to this elegant but easy to prepare dish.

Georgia Peach Glazed Pork Ribs and Onions

2 lbs. boneless pork ribs
2 cloves garlic, minced
¼ c. oil
4 sm. onions, quartered
¾ c. peach preserves
2 T. peach schnapps

Salt and pepper pork ribs and place in roasting pan. Combine garlic and oil and brush ribs on all sides. Cover and bake in 425° oven for 30 minutes. Remove cover, place onions around pork and baste onions with some of pan drippings. Bake 20 minutes. Combine preserves with schnapps and begin basting pork and onions with mixture every 10 minutes for the next 40 minutes or until desired tenderness.

Note: All you need to add to this down home Georgia favorite is fresh corn on the cob, potato salad and FRIENDS!!

Southern Collard Rolls

¼ c. finely chopped bell pepper
¼ c. finely chopped onion
¼ c. finely chopped celery
Oil
1½ c. cornbread crumbs
¾ lb. ground pork
¼ tsp. ground red pepper
1 egg
½ tsp. salt
12 med. collard leaves, stem removed and blanched
1 (15-oz.) can chicken broth
½ c. sliced onions

Sauté pepper, onion and celery in small amount of oil until tender. Set aside. In medium mixing bowl, combine cornbread crumbs, pork, ground red pepper, egg and salt. Mix well. Add onion mixture and blend in. Divide meat mixture into 12 portions and place 1 portion in center of each collard leaf. Roll in egg roll fashion and secure with toothpick. Place seam side down in casserole dish. Pour half of the chicken broth over rolls. Layer sliced onions over top. Bake in 400° oven covered for 1 hour. Add additional broth as needed during cooking so that rolls do not dry out.

Note: This Southern dish stands alone or can be nestled around a succulent pork roast for a hearty meal.

River Road Ham Cakes

¼ c. minced onion
¼ c. minced bell peppers
2 T. chopped pimiento pepper
1½ c. very finely chopped, cooked ham
⅓ c. plus ½ c. cracker crumbs
⅓ c. mayonnaise
2 T. mustard
Salt and pepper to taste
Oil

Sauté onion and pepper 5 minutes. Add pimiento and sauté until all is tender. Remove from heat and set aside. In mixing bowl, combine ham, ⅓ cup cracker crumbs, mayonnaise, mustard, salt and pepper. Form into patties, dividing mixture evenly. Dredge in ½ cup cracker crumbs. Refrigerate ½ hour or until well chilled. Heat ½ inch of oil in skillet and brown on both sides over medium-high heat for 5 to 7 minutes.

Note: For weekend guests, make these ahead and keep covered in refrigerator until ready to cook. They are excellent as the base for eggs Benedict or perfect for lunch or dinner with potato salad or mac 'n cheese.

Sausage Apple Bake

4 c. day-old crumbled cornbread
¼ c. chopped bell pepper
¼ c. chopped onion
¼ c. chopped celery
1 tsp. ground sage
¾ tsp. salt
1 tsp. black pepper
1 egg
2 T. oil
½ c. milk
1 lb. ground pork sausage
2 lg. apples, cored and sliced
3 tsp. brown sugar

In large mixing bowl, combine cornbread, bell pepper, onion, celery, sage, salt and pepper. Mix well. Add egg, oil and milk. When thoroughly mixed, blend sausage in. When combined, place in a greased 2-quart casserole. Layer apples on top. Sprinkle with brown sugar. Cover and bake at 400° for 45 minutes. Remove cover and continue baking 15 minutes longer.

Note: On a crisp autumn evening, serve this with creamy coleslaw and a hot cup of corn chowder. Makes the perfect meal to have in the family room with your favorite movie.

Mustard Crusted Pepper Coated Ham Steaks

4 ham steaks, ½ inch thick
¼ c. brown sugar
3 T. yellow prepared mustard
1 c. fine cracker crumbs
1 T. coarse ground black pepper
4 tsp. butter

Place ham steaks on greased baking sheet. In small mixing bowl, combine brown sugar and mustard. Divide mixture between steaks heavily basting top of each steak. In separate mixing bowl, blend crumbs and black pepper. Pat crumb mixture onto ham steaks, covering entire top surface of steaks. Place 1 teaspoon butter on top of each steak. Bake in 350° oven for 45 minutes, or until golden brown.

Note: Mama made this recipe one winter night for supper. She served it with creamy mashed potatoes and buttered corn. We loved it!

Papa's Salisbury Steak Supreme

¾ lb. ground sirloin
¾ lb. ground pork
1 egg
1 tsp. salt
1 tsp. black pepper
½ tsp. garlic powder
1 med. onion, very thinly sliced
⅓ c. flour
Oil for frying
6 slices bacon, fried and crumbled

In medium mixing bowl, thoroughly combine sirloin, pork, egg, salt, black pepper and garlic powder. Blend very well. Form into ½-inch thick patties. Place on baking sheet and place under broiler and cook to desired doneness. While patties are broiling, separate onion into rings and dredge in flour. Heat oil in skillet and drop onion rings in frying until golden brown and crisp. Drain on paper towel. When steaks are done, top with crumbled bacon and fried onion rings.

Note: On Dad's night in the kitchen, you were always in for a pleasant surprise. He created this recipe himself.

DEEP SOUTH BOURBON GLAZED BURGERS

4 slices bacon
1 sm. onion, chopped
1 c. shredded sharp cheddar cheese
1½ lbs. ground beef
1 tsp. salt
1 tsp. black pepper
¾ tsp. garlic powder
½ c. hickory barbecue sauce
1 clove garlic, minced
2 T. Kentucky bourbon

In skillet, fry bacon until crisp and drain on paper towels. In 2 tablespoons of the bacon grease, fry onion until tender. Remove from skillet and cool. In small bowl, combine bacon, onion and cheese and set aside. In medium bowl, blend beef, salt, pepper and garlic powder. Divide meat mixture into 8 equal portions. Press until patties are ¼ inch thick. On 4 of the patties, place ¼ of the cheese bacon mixture. Top each patty with remaining 4 patties. Crimp edges to seal. Place in large skillet or over hot coals. While cooking patties, combine sauce, garlic and bourbon in small bowl. After cooking patties 5 to 7 minutes on each side, begin basting with bourbon sauce. Frequently baste each side until burgers reach desired doneness.

Note: Get a cold drink and gather 'round the open pit for these mouth-watering burgers. Grab one hot off the grill, place on a toasted bun with slices of onion and tomato and woof it down. They're great!

LOW COUNTRY SURF 'N TURF BURGERS

¼ c. chopped red pepper
¼ c. chopped onion
2 T. margarine
1 (6-oz.) can lump crab meat, drained
1 clove garlic, minced
¼ tsp. cayenne pepper
4 oz. cream cheese, softened
1½ lbs. ground sirloin
1 tsp. salt
1 tsp. black pepper
4 slices sharp cheddar
4 ciabatta rolls, split
4 T. green tomato relish

Sauté red pepper and onion in margarine until tender. Remove from heat, add crabmeat, garlic and cayenne pepper. Cool. Blend in cream cheese and set aside. Divide sirloin into 8 equal portions and shape into patties ¼ inch thick. Place ¼ of the crab mixture on each of 4 of the patties. Top with remaining 4 patties. Crimp edges to seal. Season with salt and pepper. Place over hot coals on grill or in large skillet on stove top. Cook until desired doneness. Place cheese on top and let melt. Place a patty on each ciabatta roll and top with green tomato relish.

Note: Surprise your hubby with a low country twist on a steak house favorite. After a hard day at work, he'll love them with his favorite drink.

"UPTOWN" GOURMET STUFFED BURGERS

1½ lbs. ground beef
¾ tsp. garlic powder
¾ tsp. salt
½ tsp. black pepper
½ tsp. ground red pepper
2 T. milk
4 oz. cream cheese, softened
¼ c. chopped green olives
¾ tsp. finely minced garlic
½ c. shredded sharp cheddar cheese

In mixing bowl, combine ground beef, garlic powder, salt, black pepper, red pepper and milk. Mix thoroughly and divide into 8 equal portions. Shape into patties 4 inches in diameter. Set aside. In separate bowl, thoroughly blend cream cheese, olives, garlic and cheddar cheese. Divide cheese mixture equally between 4 of the patties. Place remaining 4 patties on top of cheese. Press down and crimp edges with fingers to seal. Grill or broil until desired doneness.

Note: You don't need to dress and go uptown to enjoy a gourmet treat. Gather around the kitchen table with friends for a "night on the town."

GEORGIA SUPER DAWGS

2 T. butter
4 hot dog buns
8 jumbo hot dogs
Mustard
16 oz. Kosher-style sauerkraut
4 T. mayonnaise
½ c. French-fried onions
4 slices bacon, fried crisp and crumbled

Butter opened hot dog buns with ½ tablespoon of butter per bun. Place buttered buns on lower rack of oven while broiling hot dogs 6 inches from broiler until toasty brown. To assemble, place 2 dogs on each bun. Top with a generous amount of mustard. Follow with 4 ounces sauerkraut per dog, then 1 tablespoon of mayonnaise dolloped on kraut. Finish with 2 tablespoons onions and 1 slice crumbled bacon on each.

Note: Ice cold ginger ale or beer is all you need with these "dawgs" and you're set for the game!

Low Country Pizza

Pizza Dough:

1 c. flour
1 c. cornmeal
½ tsp. garlic powder
1 pkg. quick-rise yeast

¼ tsp. salt
1 T. oil
¾ to 1 c. warm water

Combine flour, cornmeal, garlic powder, yeast and salt. Add oil and water and mix until blended and forms soft dough. Cover and let rise until double. Grease 16-inch pizza pan. When dough is raised, spread with hands in pan and top with pizza ingredients.

1 (16-inch) pizza crust
½ c. pizza sauce
6 oz. andouille sausage, sliced ⅛ inch thick
½ c. chopped bell pepper
1 med. onion, sliced thin

½ c. thin sliced okra
½ c. chopped shrimp
1 tsp. garlic powder
¼ c. Parmesan cheese, grated
4 oz. grated Pepper Jack cheese

Preheat oven to 450°. Spread pizza sauce over crust. Top with sausage, bell pepper, onion, okra and shrimp. Sprinkle with garlic powder and Parmesan cheese. Bake 20 to 25 minutes. Remove from oven and top with Pepper Jack cheese. Return to oven for 10 minutes or until bubbly and melted.

Note: Saturday night is "pizza night" at our house. It's been a family tradition for 60 years. This version is especially good with a tossed salad and, of course, a movie!!

Breads and Biscuits

Helpful Hints

- When baking bread, a small dish of water in the oven will keep the crust from getting too hard or brown.
- Use shortening, not margarine or oil, to grease pans when baking bread. Margarine and oil absorb more readily into the dough.
- To make self-rising flour, mix 4 cups flour, 2 teaspoons salt, and 2 tablespoons baking powder. Store in a tightly covered container.
- One scant tablespoon of bulk yeast is equal to one packet of yeast.
- Hot water kills yeast. One way to test for the correct temperature is to pour the water over your wrist. If you cannot feel hot or cold, the temperature is just right.
- When in doubt, always sift flour before measuring.
- Use bread flour for baking heavier breads, such as mixed grain, pizza doughs, bagels, etc.
- When baking in a glass pan, reduce the oven temperature by 25°.
- When baking bread, you can achieve a finer texture if you use milk. Water makes a coarser bread.
- Fill an empty salt shaker with flour to quickly and easily dust a bread pan or work surface.
- For successful quick breads, do not overmix the dough. Mix only until combined. An overmixed batter creates tough and rubbery muffins, biscuits, and quick breads.
- Muffins can be eaten warm. Most other quick breads taste better the next day. Nut breads are better if stored 24 hours before serving.
- Nuts, shelled or unshelled, keep best and longest when stored in the freezer. Unshelled nuts crack more easily when frozen. Nuts can be used directly from the freezer.
- Enhance the flavor of nuts, such as almonds, walnuts, and pecans, by toasting them before using in recipes. Place nuts on a baking sheet and bake at 300° for 5–8 minutes or until slightly browned.
- Overripe bananas can be frozen until it's time to bake. Store them unpeeled in a plastic bag.
- The freshness of eggs can be tested by placing them in a large bowl of cold water; if they float, do not use them.

Breads And Biscuits

Country Peach Bread

½ c. butter, softened
½ c. sugar
½ c. brown sugar
3 eggs
2¾ c. flour
1½ tsp. baking powder
½ tsp. baking soda
1 tsp. salt
2 c. diced fresh peaches
3 T. peach nectar
1 tsp. vanilla extract

Cream butter and sugars. Add eggs, one at a time, beating well after each egg. In separate bowl, combine flour, baking powder, baking soda and salt. Add dry ingredients to creamed mixture alternately with peaches. Stir in nectar and vanilla. Pour batter into greased and floured 9 x 5-inch loaf pan. Bake at 350° for 1 hour or until tests done when wooden pick inserted in center comes out clean. Cool 10 minutes. Remove from pan and cool completely before serving.

Note: For a summer morning breakfast, serve this with whipped butter, crispy fried bacon and hot coffee or tea.

Southern Bacon Cheddar Bread

3 c. flour
1 tsp. salt
1 T. sugar
1 pkg. yeast
1 c. warm milk
1 T. oil
¾ c. grated cheddar cheese
4 slices bacon, fried crisp and crumbled

In large mixing bowl, blend flour, salt and sugar. In separate bowl, stir yeast into warm milk along with oil until dissolved. Pour into flour mixture and mix well. Place dough into well greased bowl. Turn so that top will be greased. Cover with kitchen towel and let rise in warm place for an hour or until double in size. When raised, place on floured work surface. Sprinkle with cheese and bacon and knead into the dough until evenly distributed. Place in a 9 x 5-inch greased bread pan. Cover and let rise in warm place until double in size. Bake in preheated 375° oven for 45 minutes or until golden brown.

Note: For a real treat, serve hot from the oven with fresh salted butter.

Bacon 'n Onion Golden Cornbread

2 slices bacon, fried and crumbled
⅓ c. chopped onion
1½ c. yellow cornmeal
½ c. flour
1 T. baking powder
1 tsp. salt
2 T. sugar
1 c. buttermilk
2 T. oil
1 egg
½ c. canned whole kernel corn, drained

In small skillet, fry bacon until crisp. Drain on paper towel. Pour off bacon fat reserving 1 tablespoon. In reserved fat, fry onion until golden but not brown. Remove from skillet and set aside. In medium mixing bowl, combine cornmeal, flour, baking powder, salt and sugar. Mix well. Add buttermilk, oil and egg. Mix well until batter is completely blended. Crumble bacon slices into batter. Add onion and whole kernel corn. Mix well. Pour into well greased pan (preferably and 8-inch iron skillet) and bake in preheated 425° oven for 20 to 25 minutes or until golden brown and tests done. Serve piping hot.

Note: Be sure to have a pan of this ready next time Peppered Greens are on your menu. And for those cold, rainy evenings, it's delicious with a steaming bowl of bean soup.

Toasted Pecan and Brown Sugar Biscuits

2 c. flour
⅓ c. brown sugar
1 T. baking powder
1 tsp. salt
⅓ c. all-vegetable shortening
⅔ c. milk
⅓ c. chopped, toasted pecans
Butter, melted
Granulated sugar

In mixing bowl, combine flour, brown sugar, baking powder and salt. Mix well. Cut in shortening until mixture resembles coarse crumbs. Make a well and add milk. Mix well until soft ball forms and dough pulls away from sides of bowl. Turn onto floured surface and sprinkle with toasted pecans. Knead 10 to 12 times working nuts into dough evenly. Press or roll out to ½ inch thick and cut with 1½-inch biscuit cutter. Bake on cookie sheet in 400° preheated oven for 20 minutes. Five minutes before cooking time is over, brush tops and sides with melted butter and sprinkle tops with granulated sugar. Return to oven until cooking time is up.

Note: Try these with slivered smoked ham at your next bunch. They're also delectable when served with clotted cream for tea time.

PINKY'S OLD TIME "SWEET BISCUITS"

4 lg. buttermilk biscuits, left over   Old-fashioned pancake syrup

Using the handle to a wooden mixing spoon, make a hole down into each biscuit but being careful not to go completely through the biscuit. Slowly drizzle syrup into the hole giving it time to soak in as you pour. Wrap each biscuit in waxed paper or aluminum foil and let set for 2 hours or longer.

Note: Pinky was the family cook and the nanny to my Dad and his brother. This was one of the sweet treats she made for them during the Depression. When they came home from school, they would find them in the warmer of the old wood stove.

TOASTED PECAN AND CHIVE BISCUITS

2 c. all-purpose flour
1 T. baking powder
1 tsp. salt
⅓ c. vegetable shortening

⅓ c. milk
⅓ c. buttermilk
¼ c. chopped, toasted pecans
1½ T. chopped chives

In mixing bowl, combine flour, baking powder and salt. Cut in shortening with fork to form coarse crumbs. Add milk, buttermilk, pecans and chives. Mix until a soft dough. Form dough into a ball. Place on lightly floured surface. Knead 8 to 10 times. Roll ½ inch thick. Cut with floured 2-inch biscuit cutter. Place on ungreased baking sheet. Bake in preheated 425° oven 12 to 15 minutes or until golden.

Note: These biscuits go great with scrambled eggs and sausages, are delicious for serving with southern fried chicken and if cut with a smaller cutter, they're excellent for afternoon tea when served with fruit butters or jams.

Recipe Favorites

Desserts and Beverages

Helpful Hints

- Keep eggs at room temperature to create greater volume when whipping egg whites for meringue.

- Pie dough can be frozen. Roll dough out between sheets of plastic wrap, stack in a pizza box, and keep the box in the freezer. Defrost in the fridge and use as needed. Use within 2 months.

- Place your pie plate on a cake stand when ready to flute the edges of the pie. The cake stand will make it easier to turn the pie plate, and you won't have to stoop over.

- When making decorative pie edges, use a spoon for a scalloped edge. Use a fork to make crosshatched and herringbone patterns.

- When cutting butter into flour for pastry dough, the process is easier if you cut the butter into small pieces before adding it to the flour.

- Pumpkin and other custard-style pies are done when they jiggle slightly in the middle. Fruit pies are done when the pastry is golden, juices bubble, and fruit is tender.

- Keep the cake plate clean while frosting by sliding 6-inch strips of waxed paper under each side of the cake. Once the cake is frosted and the frosting is set, pull the strips away, leaving a clean plate.

- Create a quick decorating tube to ice your cake with chocolate. Put chocolate in a heat-safe, zipper-lock plastic bag. Immerse it in simmering water until the chocolate is melted. Snip off the tip of one corner, and squeeze the chocolate out of the bag.

- Achieve professionally decorated cakes with a silky, molten look by blow-drying the frosting with a hair dryer until the frosting melts slightly.

- To ensure that you have equal amounts of batter in each pan when making a layered cake, use a kitchen scale to measure the weight.

- Prevent cracking in your cheesecake by placing a shallow pan of hot water on the bottom oven rack and keeping the oven door shut during baking.

- A cheesecake needs several hours to chill and set.

- For a perfectly cut cheesecake, dip the knife into hot water and clean it after each cut. You can also hold a length of dental floss taut and pull it down through the cheesecake to make a clean cut across the diameter of the cake.

Desserts And Beverages

CHOCOLATE PECAN PIE WITH ORANGE CREAM

3 eggs
⅔ c. sugar
¼ tsp. salt
1 c. dark corn syrup
1 tsp. vanilla
⅓ c. butter, melted
1 c. chopped pecans

2 T. chocolate chips
1 (9-inch) unbaked pie shell
½ c. pecan halves
½ c. heavy whipping cream
1½ T. powdered sugar
¼ tsp. vanilla
⅛ tsp. orange extract

Beat eggs thoroughly with sugar, salt, corn syrup, vanilla and butter. Add chopped pecans and chocolate chips. Pour into pie shell and arrange pecan halves on top. Bake in 350° oven 50 minutes or until knife inserted halfway between center and edge comes out clean. Cool. Meanwhile, in medium mixing bowl, beat cream until soft peaks form. Add powdered sugar, vanilla and orange extract and continue beating until stiff peaks form. When serving pie, top each slice with dollop of orange cream.

Note: This is a good dessert after a night of hamburgers, just like going to the diner.

Banana Custard Pie with Pecan Praline Sauce

Banana Custard Pie;

1 (9-inch) pie shell, unbaked
4 eggs
½ c. sugar
1 tsp. vanilla
½ tsp. salt

1½ c. milk
1 c. half-and-half
1 c. sliced bananas
½ tsp. cinnamon

Bake pie shell 5 minutes in 450° oven. Set aside. In large mixing bowl, lightly beat eggs. Stir in sugar, vanilla and salt. Gradually stir in milk and half-and-half. Add bananas and cinnamon. Pour into pie shell and bake at 350° for 40 to 45 minutes being careful that the edges do not burn. Cover edges with foil, if necessary. When pie is set, remove from oven. Cool and serve with sauce.

Pecan Praline Sauce:

¼ c. butter
¾ c. brown sugar
1 tsp. vanilla

½ c. chopped pecans, toasted
¼ tsp. salt

In small skillet, melt butter and sugar together. Stir in vanilla, nuts and salt and cook until caramelized and serve over pie slices.

Note: Not much time left? In a hurry but want a scrumptious dessert? This is it!

Blackberry Walnut Crumb Pie

1 qt. fresh blackberries, washed and drained
1½ c. sugar
⅛ tsp. salt
1½ T. flour
1 (9-inch) pie shell, unbaked

3 T. butter or margarine
⅓ c. brown sugar
⅔ c. flour
¼ tsp. salt
¼ c. chopped walnuts

In mixing bowl, mix blackberries with sugar, salt and flour. Fill pie shell with berry mixture. In small mixing bowl, cut butter or margarine into sugar, flour and salt to form coarse crumbs. Stir in walnuts. Sprinkle crumb mixture over top of filling making sure that crumb covers all the way to edge of crust. Bake at 450° for 10 minutes. Reduce heat to 350° and bake 25 minutes longer or until crumb is golden brown and blackberry syrup begins to bubble up.

Note: In the warm summer days in the South, our blackberries just flourish. Fresh picked berries make this pie a family favorite.

SALTED PEANUT-CARAMEL ICE CREAM PIE

1½ c. graham cracker crumbs
¼ c. finely chopped peanuts
½ tsp. salt
2 tsp. sugar
6 T. butter, melted

1 qt. vanilla ice cream, softened
¼ c. finely chopped salted, toasted peanuts
6 T. caramel ice cream topping
¼ tsp. sea salt

In mixing bowl, combine graham cracker crumbs, peanuts, salt and sugar. Mix well. Add melted butter and mix with fork until moistened. Press crumb mixture in bottom and up sides of 9-inch pie dish. Bake in 350° oven for 5 minutes. Cool completely. Spoon softened ice cream into crust. Smooth top with back of spoon. Sprinkle with toasted peanuts then finely drizzle caramel topping over peanuts and sprinkle with sea salt. Place in freezer for 4 hours or overnight.

Note: This salty sweet dessert is an excellent way to end a summer evening barbecue.

PINKY'S ICEBOX PUDDIN'

1 pt. heavy whipping cream
4 T. powdered sugar

1 tsp. vanilla
60 chocolate snaps

In large bowl, whip cream until stiff adding sugar while whipping. Fold in vanilla. Using small casserole dish, line bottom with ⅓ of the snaps. Spread ⅓ of whipped cream over snaps covering to edge. Repeat layers, ending with whipped cream. Cover and refrigerate at least 4 hours or for better results, overnight.

Note: This dessert was one of my Dad's favorites when he was growing up. Pinky, the family cook created it, it's so simple and so delicious and so typical of the "icebox" desserts that were popular in the 1930's.

RIVER ROAD BREAD PUDDING WITH BOURBON SAUCE

4 lg. eggs, separated
2 c. milk
1 c. sugar
½ tsp. salt
1 T. vanilla

½ tsp. cinnamon
¼ c. butter, melted
5 c. day-old bread cubes
½ c. crushed pineapple, drained
Bourbon Sauce

Butter a 2-quart casserole dish and set aside. In medium mixing bowl, beat egg whites until stiff and glossy. Set aside. In large mixing bowl, whisk together egg yolks, milk, sugar, salt, vanilla, cinnamon and butter. Add bread cubes and toss well. Let stand 5 minutes. Fold in pineapple and gently fold in egg whites. Pour into casserole and bake in preheated 375° oven for 35 to 40 minutes or until tests done.

Bourbon Sauce:

3 T. butter
1 c. brown sugar

3 T. bourbon
¾ tsp. vanilla

In skillet, melt butter. Add brown sugar and cook, stirring until dissolved and is making a syrup. Remove from heat. Add bourbon and vanilla. Return to heat and cook 5 to 7 minutes longer. Serve warm over bread pudding.

Note: Having a good old Southern get-together? Serve this mouth-watering bread pudding as a way to end a perfect meal.

BANANAS FOSTER CRISPY RICE BARS

¼ c. margarine
1 (10-oz.) pkg. caramel flavored marshmallows
¼ tsp. banana extract

⅛ tsp. rum extract
6½ c. crispy rice cereal
1 c. vanilla candy melts

In large saucepan, melt margarine and marshmallows. When melted, stir banana and rum extracts. Remove from heat and stir in rice cereal stirring to coat evenly. Spread into greased 11 x 9-inch pan. Let cool then cut into 2 x 3-inch bars. In small pan over pot of boiling water, melt vanilla candy melts until soft. Drizzle desired amounts over bars and let cool.

Note: Favorite Southern flavors blend nicely into this all-time favorite, crispy rice bars.

SOUTHERN "PEANUT LOG" CRISPIE BARS

1 T. margarine
5 c. mini marshmallows
2 T. creamy peanut butter
6 c. crispy rice cereal
½ c. marshmallow creme
¼ c. chopped peanuts

In saucepan, melt margarine and marshmallows, stirring constantly until smooth. Stir in peanut butter. When peanut butter is blended in, add the rice cereal. Stir until thoroughly combined. In 13 x 9-inch greased pan, place half the mixture. Press down until even and compressed. Spread marshmallow creme over mixture and sprinkle with peanuts. Turn rest of mixture into pan, even out and press down until level and smooth. Let cool and cut into 1½-inch wide bars.

Note: Anyone from the South remembers old-fashioned peanut logs. These crispie bars have the same "old time" taste and make great lunch box treats for kids and hubby.

BLACKBERRY PATCH BARS

1 c. flour
1 c. uncooked rolled oats
⅓ c. brown sugar, packed
½ tsp. baking soda
¼ tsp. salt
½ c. margarine
⅔ c. seedless blackberry preserves
¼ c. chopped, toasted walnuts
2 T. brown sugar

In mixing bowl, combine flour, oats, brown sugar, baking soda and salt. Cut margarine in until mixture is crumbly. Press half of crumb mixture into bottom of 8-inch square baking pan, greased. Spread preserves evenly to within ½ inch of crust. Sprinkle with remaining crumb mixture. Top with walnuts and lightly press down on top of crumb mixture. Sprinkle with brown sugar. Bake in preheated 350° oven for 25 minutes or until light golden brown. Cool completely and cut into bars.

Note: Peter Rabbit never had anything this good! So easy to make and your little bunnies will love them.

MACON CHERRY BLOSSOMS

1 c. butter, softened
½ c. confectioners' sugar
½ tsp. vanilla
½ tsp. almond extract
¼ tsp. salt
¼ c. drained and chopped maraschino cherries

2¼ c. flour
¾ c. finely chopped almonds
1 c. pink confectioners' sugar (available in gourmet specialty shops)

Preheat oven to 400°. In large bowl, cream together butter and sugar. Beat until fluffy. Add vanilla, almond extract, salt and cherries. Mix well. Gradually stir in flour. Next stir in chopped nuts. Shape dough into 1-inch balls. Place on ungreased cookie sheet. Bake 12 to 14 minutes until set; do not brown. Remove from baking sheet and cool for a few minutes. While still warm, roll in pink sugar to coat. Place on rack to cool. Then roll once again in pink sugar.

Note: I was inspired to create this recipe when visiting Macon, GA in cherry blossom time. They make a beautiful and tasty center piece on your dessert table.

DONUT SHOP SHORTCAKE

1 c. sliced fresh strawberries
1 T. sugar
4 old-fashioned glazed donuts

1 pt. strawberry ice cream
Whipped cream

In mixing bowl, toss strawberries and sugar and set aside. Place donuts on individual serving plates. Top each donut with scoop of strawberry ice cream. Spoon fresh strawberries over ice cream and top with desired amount of whipped cream.

Note: In the good old summertime, enjoy this new twist on an old favorite.

SOUTHERN PRALINE CREAM CAKE

1 (9-inch) loaf store-bought pound cake
1 pt. butter pecan ice cream, semi-softened
1 c. heavy whipping cream
2 T. powdered sugar
1 T. bourbon
¼ c. caramel sauce
¼ c. chopped pecans, toasted

Split pound cake in half lengthwise. Spoon ice cream evenly over bottom half of cake. Top with top half of cake and place in freezer. In small mixing bowl, whip cream until soft peaks form. Add sugar and bourbon and continue whipping until stiff. Remove cake from freezer and frost entire cake with whipped cream. Drizzle caramel sauce in crisscross pattern over top of cake. Sprinkle with toasted pecans. Return to freezer until ready to serve.

Note: Serve this easy-to-make dessert on a lazy Sunday afternoon on the veranda. Mmm Mmm, Southern sweets at their best!

SUMMER PEACH CHEESECAKE WITH GINGER CRUST

2 c. firmly packed gingersnap crumbs
⅓ c. sugar
6 T. butter, melted
4 (8-oz.) pkgs. cream cheese, softened
1¼ c. sugar
5 lg. eggs
2 T. flour
1 (8-oz.) ctn. sour cream
1 c. fresh peach slices, drained on paper towels and patted dry
½ c. apricot jam, melted

In a small bowl, combine gingersnap crumbs, sugar and butter. Press firmly on bottom and up sides of 9½-inch springform pan. Bake 10 minutes in preheated 300° oven. Set aside to cool. In large mixing bowl, beat cream cheese and sugar with an electric mixer on medium speed until fluffy. Beat in eggs, one at a time, beating well after each egg is added. Add flour; beat 1 minute. Stir in sour cream. Spoon batter into crust. Bake 1 hour 15 minutes in preheated 300° oven. Turn oven off. Let stand in oven with door closed for 4 hours. Remove from oven. Gently run knife blade around edge to release. Cool completely in pan. Cover and chicken 8 hours or overnight. An hour before serving, arrange peach slices in desired pattern on top of cheesecake. Carefully spoon melted jam over peach slices to glaze, being careful not to saturate edges of cake with jam. Chill 1 hour before serving.

Note: In the good old summertime, you can't beat this with a pot of hot tea and a breezy front porch.

Peanut Butter and Jam Cheesecake

2 (8-oz.) pkgs. cream cheese, softened
⅔ c. sugar
2 T. creamy peanut butter
1 tsp. vanilla
2 eggs
1 (9-inch) graham cracker crust
½ c. strawberry or grape jam

In large mixing bowl, beat cream cheese, sugar, peanut butter and vanilla until fluffy. Add eggs, one at a time, and beat until well mixed. Place graham cracker crust on baking sheet. Pour in cream cheese mixture and bake in preheated 350° oven for 25 to 30 minutes or until set. Remove from oven, let cool for 1 hour, then spread jam on top. Chill well before serving.

Note: For the peanut butter fans at your house, surprise them with this delicious cheesecake. A new twist on an old favorite.

Quick Bread Pudding

3 lg. eggs
1 c. milk
1 tsp. vanilla
¼ c. brown sugar
½ tsp. salt
3 c. day-old cinnamon-raisin bread, cubed
2 T. margarine, melted

In large mixing bowl, beat eggs and milk together. Add vanilla, brown sugar and salt. Add bread cubes and margarine to egg mixture. Let stand 5 to 10 minutes. Lightly grease 1-quart casserole. Pour mixture into casserole and bake in preheated 350° oven for 35 to 45 minutes or until tests done.

Note: Out shopping? Got home late? No dessert for tonight? Mix up this bread pudding in just minutes. The family will love it!

CHATTAHOOCHEE RIVER BLACKBERRY COBBLER

4 c. fresh blackberries
1 c. sugar
2½ T. cornstarch
Pinch of salt
1 c. flour
1 T. sugar

1½ tsp. baking powder
¼ tsp. salt
½ c. milk
⅓ c. butter, melted
Sugar

In large bowl, combine berries, sugar and cornstarch and salt, tossing to coat berries evenly. Place berries into 1½-quart baking dish. Set aside. In bowl, combine flour, sugar, baking powder and salt. Add milk and butter and mix until dry ingredients are moist. Drop tablespoons of batter evenly over the berries. Sprinkle with sugar over top. Bake in preheated 375° oven until golden brown, 20 minutes or more or until fruit is bubbly. Cool or serve warm.

Note: Back during the Depression when Daddy was just a boy, blackberries grew wild down by the banks of the Chattahoochee River. He and my uncle would pick buckets full for Pinky, the cook, to make pies and cobblers.

FRIED APPLE STICKS

¾ c. pancake mix
¾ c. water
1 c. cracker crumbs
½ tsp. cinnamon

2 lg. apples, peeled, cored and sliced into sticks
Vegetable oil

Combine pancake mix with water until smooth. In separate bowl, mix cracker crumbs and cinnamon. Dip apple sticks in batter mix and dredge in crumb mixture. Fry in hot oil until golden brown. Drain on paper towels.

Note: While these are still warm, they can be rolled in sifted confectioners' sugar.

Raisin Cheese Pastry

1 (8-oz.) pkg. cream cheese
½ c. ricotta cheese
1 egg
1 egg yolk
½ c. sugar
1 tsp. vanilla

½ tsp. lemon extract
½ tsp. cinnamon
½ c. raisins
½ c. toasted, chopped walnuts
1 sheet frozen puff pastry, thawed
1 egg, beaten

In mixing bowl, combine cream cheese, ricotta cheese, egg and egg yolk, sugar, vanilla, lemon extract and cinnamon. Mix until smooth. Fold in raisins and nuts. Set aside. On floured surface, roll pastry sheet to ⅛-inch thickness. Spread filling in center of pastry. Brush edges of pastry with beaten egg. Fold ends over and roll in egg roll fashion. Place seam side down on baking sheet. Brush with beaten egg and bake in preheated at 350° oven for 20 minutes or until puffed and golden brown. Let cool before serving.

Note: Be sure to have a hot pot of coffee or tea ready when you serve this fresh baked delight!

Autumn Pumpkin Puffs

2 sheets frozen puff pastry dough, thawed
1 egg
6 oz. cream cheese, softened
¾ c. canned pumpkin
¼ c. sugar

¼ c. brown sugar
1 tsp. cinnamon
½ tsp. nutmeg
1 tsp. vanilla
½ tsp. salt
Confectioners' sugar for dusting

On lightly floured surface, roll pastry sheets to ⅛-inch thickness. Using 4-inch round cutter, cut 12 circles. Place 6 of the circles on parchment-lined baking sheet and set aside. In a small bowl, beat egg and set aside. In medium mixing bowl, combine cream cheese, pumpkin, sugar, brown sugar, cinnamon, nutmeg, vanilla and salt. Beat until smooth. On 6 rounds on baking sheet, place 3 teaspoons of pumpkin filling in center of each round. Brush edges with beaten egg. Top filled rounds with remaining 6 cut rounds. Crimp edges with fork to seal. Brush surface of each puff with egg. Bake in preheated 350° oven for 20 minutes or until puffed and golden. Remove from oven, cool and dust with confectioners' sugar.

Note: A hot pot of coffee and a platter of fresh baked pumpkin puffs. A great afternoon treat.

PAPA'S BACON-PEACH MUNCHIES

8 egg roll wrappers
½ c. peach jam
1 c. sliced peaches
1 lb. breakfast bacon, fried crisp and drained
1 egg, lightly beaten
Oil for frying

Separate egg roll wrappers. In small bowl, combine peach jam and sliced peaches. Divide among egg roll wrappers placing in center of each. Top with 2 strips of bacon on each. Roll egg roll fashion and seal edges by brushing with beaten egg. Fry in hot oil until golden brown. Drain on paper towels.

Note: Papa always liked to get in the kitchen and create little treats for the family. These really disappear quick at the table. Sometimes they never make it that far!

SPARKLING PINK LEMONADE

½ gal. pink lemonade, chilled
2 c. pink champagne, chilled
¼ c. pink sugar
Thin sliced lemon

Just before serving, combine lemonade and champagne. Using a wedge of lemon, rim the glasses with lemon juice and dredge in saucer of pink sugar. Top each glass rim with a slice of lemon.

Note: This refreshing beverage is intended for adults only. It's quite sparkly and very spiked!

RASPBERRY LIME FIZZLE

1 pt. lime sherbet
1 L. raspberry flavored ginger ale, chilled
½ pt. fresh raspberries
1 lime, thinly sliced

For each drink, place 1 scoop of lime sherbet in a chilled daiquiri glass. Pour ginger ale over sherbet. Skewer fresh raspberries and place 1 skewer in each glass. Trim edge of glass with lime slice.

Note: Nothing could be more refreshing on a scorching hot summer afternoon!

SOUTHERN SWEET CITRUS TEA

2 qt. water
10 to 12 tea bags
½ c. sugar or to taste
1 c. orange juice

1 c. tangerine juice
¼ c. lemon juice
Sliced lemons
Sliced oranges

To boiling water, add tea bags and sugar. Remove from heat and let cool. Remove tea bags. Add orange juice, tangerine juice and lemon juice. Serve over crushed ice and garnish with orange or lemon slices.

Note: This is not your ordinary Southern sweet tea. This one was kissed by the Sunshine state.

GINGER PEACHY CREAM SODAS

1 fresh peach, peeled, diced and puréed
2 tsp. sugar
4 oz. heavy cream

1 (2 L.) ginger ale, chilled
1 qt. peach ice cream
Whipped topping
4 peach slices

Combine puréed peaches and sugar. Divide between 4 soda glasses. To each glass, add 1 ounce heavy cream and muddle. Then pour each glass ⅓ full of ginger ale. Add 2 scoops of ice cream to each glass. Finish filling glasses with ginger ale using a fine stream. Top with whipped topping and peach slice.

Note: It's all in the name... It's ginger peachy!

Relishes, Butters and Sauces

Helpful Hints

- Never overcook foods that are to be frozen. Foods will finish cooking when reheated. Don't refreeze cooked, thawed foods.

- When freezing foods, label each container with its contents and the date it was put into the freezer. Always use frozen, cooked foods within 1–2 months.

- To avoid teary eyes when cutting onions, cut them under cold running water or briefly place them in the freezer before cutting.

- Fresh lemon juice will remove onion scent from hands.

- To get the most juice out of fresh lemons, bring them to room temperature and roll them under your palm against the kitchen counter before cutting and squeezing.

- Add raw rice to the salt shaker to keep the salt free flowing.

- Transfer jelly and salad dressings to small plastic squeeze bottles – no more messy, sticky jars!

- Ice cubes will help sharpen garbage disposal blades.

- Separate stuck-together glasses by filling the inside glass with cold water and setting both in hot water.

- Clean CorningWare® by filling it with water and dropping in two denture cleaning tablets. Let stand for 30–45 minutes.

- Always spray your grill with nonstick cooking spray before grilling to avoid sticking.

- To make a simple polish for copper bottom cookware, mix equal parts of flour and salt with vinegar to create a paste.

- Purchase a new coffee grinder and mark it "spices." It can be used to grind most spices; however, cinnamon bark, nutmeg, and others must be broken up a little first. Clean the grinder after each use.

- In a large shaker, combine 6 parts salt and 1 part pepper for quick and easy seasoning.

- Save your store-bought bread bags and ties–they make perfect storage bags for homemade bread.

- Next time you need a quick ice pack, grab a bag of frozen peas or other vegetables out of the freezer.

Relishes, Butters And Sauces

OKRA AND TOMATO RELISH

1 c. chopped pickled okra
1 (14-oz.) can stewed tomatoes,
  drained and chopped
1 clove garlic, finely minced
½ tsp. cayenne pepper
3 tsp. sugar
1 T. vinegar

In mixing bowl, combine okra, tomatoes, garlic, cayenne pepper, sugar and vinegar. Stir well to blend. For best results, make a day or two in advance.

Note: Next time you serve fried chicken for Sunday dinner be sure to set out a dish of this relish. Everyone will rave over it!

SAVORY VIDALIA PEACH RELISH

3 c. chopped fresh peaches
½ c. sugar
1 Vidalia onion, chopped
1 T. cider vinegar
4 tsp. fresh lemon juice

In large saucepan, combine peaches, sugar and onion. Bring to boil and reduce heat to simmer. Cook, stirring often until syrup begins to thicken (consistency of jam). Add vinegar and lemon juice. Cook 2 minutes longer. Remove from heat and let cool. Store in glass jars in refrigerator until ready to serve.

Note: While this is delicious served with roasted pork, for a really special treat, use as a glaze during roasting. It's also a nice touch for baked chicken.

Pineapple Relish

1 c. crushed pineapple, drained
¼ c. diced onion
2 T. diced pimiento
½ c. sugar
2 T. vinegar
½ tsp. black pepper

In medium saucepan, combine pineapple, onion, pimiento and sugar. Cook, stirring often until syrup begins to thicken (consistency of jam). Add vinegar. Cook 2 minutes longer. Remove from heat and stir in black pepper. Let cool. Store in glass jars in refrigerator.

Note: The pineapple has long been a symbol of hospitality. This relish is an excellent way to welcome guests to a scrumptious meal. Serve with baked ham or roasted chicken. Makes a great spread for sandwiches made from leftover ham.

Blackberry Relish

3 c. blackberries, fresh or frozen
1 apple, peeled and diced
¼ c. diced onion
½ c. sugar
2 tsp. cider vinegar
4 tsp. fresh lemon juice

In large saucepan, combine blackberries, apple, onion and sugar. Bring to a boil and reduce heat; simmer 5 minutes. Add vinegar and lemon juice. Stir carefully, just to mix. Remove from heat and let cool. Pour through large strainer to drain off any juice. Chill mixture and serve as relish.

Note: The sweet-tart quality of this relish will enhance roasted pork, baked chicken, or use as a spread on sandwiches.

Country Corn Relish

1 (15-oz.) can whole kernel corn, drained
2 T. chopped green bell pepper
2 T. finely chopped onion
2 T. diced pimiento
2 T. vinegar
3 T. sugar

In small saucepan, combine corn, bell pepper, onion, pimiento, vinegar and sugar. Cook over medium heat, stirring often until mixture thickens. Remove from heat; cool. Store in glass jars in refrigerator.

Note: An old time Southern favorite that is welcome on any table today.

Game Time Hot Dog and Burger Relish

1 c. dill pickle relish
¼ c. finely chopped onions
2 tsp. sugar

3 T. beer
⅓ c. mayonnaise
2 T. yellow mustard

In small saucepan, combine relish, onion, sugar and beer. Stir well and cook over medium heat until beer evaporates. Remove from heat; cool. Stir in mayonnaise and mustard. Keep covered in refrigerator.

Note: Be sure to keep plenty on hand during game season. Goes great on dogs and burgers but don't forget it on your subs!

Pimiento Cheese Butter

½ lb. butter
1 c. grated cheddar cheese

¼ c. chopped pimiento

In food processor, blend butter and cheese together until smooth. Add pimiento, pulsing, until just blended. Pack in jar or crock and refrigerate until ready to use. Allow to come to room temperature before serving.

Note: Pimiento cheese is an old Southern favorite and this butter will be a favorite of your family. Serve on baked potatoes, too!

Blackberry Butter

½ c. butter, softened
¼ c. seedless blackberry preserves

¼ tsp. lemon juice

In small bowl, blend butter, blackberry preserves and lemon juice. Mix until well blended. Store covered in refrigerator.

Note: Terrific at breakfast with hot buttermilk biscuits and crispy fried bacon. And don't forget to put some out at your next tea.

CORN-ON-THE-COB BUTTER

½ c. butter, softened
½ tsp. garlic powder
¾ tsp. onion powder
¼ tsp. cayenne pepper
¼ tsp. black pepper
¼ tsp. chili powder
¼ tsp. salt

In bowl, blend butter, garlic powder, onion powder, cayenne pepper, black pepper, chili powder and salt. Mix until well blended. Store covered in refrigerator.

Note: Next time you have a cook out, have plenty of this on hand for fresh corn on the cob. Goes great on baked potato too!

GEORGIA PEACH BUTTER

½ c. butter, softened
¼ c. peach preserves or jam
¼ tsp. lemon juice
⅛ tsp. cinnamon

In small bowl, cream butter and preserves or jam together until smooth. Stir in lemon juice and cinnamon and blend well. Cover and refrigerate until serving time.

Note: An ideal topping on buttermilk biscuits at breakfast and a real treat at afternoon tea.

HOT 'N SPICY GARLIC BUTTER

½ c. butter, softened
2 cloves garlic, crushed
1 tsp. red hot sauce
½ tsp. cayenne pepper
½ tsp. paprika
¼ tsp. black pepper
¼ tsp. sea salt

In small bowl, blend butter, garlic, hot sauce, cayenne, paprika, black pepper and salt. Blend until mixed well.

Note: Perfect for a zesty garlic bread but great on baked potato or even to top off your grilled steaks.

SOUTHERN PIMIENTO CHEESE SALAD DRESSING

½ c. sour cream
¼ c. mayonnaise
¼ c. prepared pimiento cheese spread
½ tsp. onion powder
1 T. chopped green olives
Milk

In mixing bowl, blend together sour cream, mayonnaise and pimiento cheese until smooth. Stir in onion powder and green olives. If mixture seems too thick, thin with milk to desired consistency. Blend well and chill until serving. Dressing can be made a day or two ahead. Keep covered in refrigerator until serving.

CREOLE MAYONNAISE

¾ c. mayonnaise
¼ tsp. minced garlic
¼ tsp. garlic powder
¼ tsp. celery seed
¼ tsp. cayenne pepper
¼ tsp. chili powder
⅛ tsp. paprika
⅛ tsp. salt
⅛ tsp. black pepper

In small mixing bowl, blend together mayonnaise, garlic, garlic powder, celery seed, cayenne pepper, chili powder, paprika, salt and pepper. Thoroughly mix until well blended. For best flavor, make 2 to 3 hours before serving.

Note: This will add Southern zest to any sandwich or burger!

LEMON-CHEESE MAYONNAISE

½ c. mayonnaise
¼ c. grated Parmesan cheese
½ tsp. fresh grated lemon peel
1 clove finely minced garlic

In small mixing bowl, combine mayonnaise, Parmesan cheese, lemon peel and garlic. Blend well. Refrigerate until serving time.

Note: For the fullest flavor, it is best to prepare this party pleasing favorite several hours or a day ahead.

CREOLE TARTAR SAUCE

½ c. mayonnaise
¼ c. hot salsa

2 T. minced green onion
¼ tsp. minced garlic

Blend mayonnaise, salsa, onion and garlic in small mixing bowl. Refrigerate until serving.

Note: An excellent sauce when you want to add a little zest to your fish dinners.

LEMON TARTAR SAUCE

½ c. mayonnaise
¼ c. dill relish
Juice of ½ lemon

1 tsp. shredded lemon peel
2 T. finely minced onion
1 tsp. sugar

Blend mayonnaise, relish, lemon juice, lemon peel, onion and sugar. Refrigerate until serving.

Note: So refreshing when served along with your favorite fried or broiled fish and seafood. It's at it's best when made days in advance.

QUICK 'N EASY OLDE SOUTH BAR-B-QUE SAUCE

2 (18-oz.) bottles hickory smoke barbecue sauce
¼ c. bourbon or moonshine
2 T. chili powder

½ c. sautéed onions, chopped
⅓ tsp. ground red pepper
½ tsp. minced garlic
1 T. brown sugar

In glass mixing bowl, combine barbecue sauce, bourbon or moonshine, chili powder, onion, red pepper, garlic and sugar. Blend well. For best results, prepare one or more days in advance. Keep refrigerated.

Note: Use this scrumptious sauce on any of your meats, beef, pork, chicken or fish. For authentic old-fashion barbecue Southern style, cook your meat 30 minutes on grill, then begin basting all sides each time you turn the meat. Be sure to use plenty of sauce when basting and grill until the sauce browns and caramelizes.

HOSPITALITY BAR-B-QUE SAUCE

1 c. ketchup
½ c. crushed pineapple, undrained
2 T. honey
1 T. bourbon

1 T. Worcestershire sauce
1 T. yellow mustard
½ tsp. minced garlic

    In mixing bowl, combine ketchup, pineapple, honey, bourbon, Worcestershire sauce, mustard and garlic. Blend well and let stand several hours before use to allow flavors to blend together.

    Note: The pineapple, a symbol of hospitality, adds a welcoming touch to this sweet and spicy sauce.

SWEET 'N SMOKY MUSTARD

8 oz. prepared yellow mustard
1½ T. sugar
¾ T. brown sugar
¾ tsp. garlic powder

¾ tsp. onion powder
1 tsp. liquid hickory smoke
¾ tsp. paprika
¾ tsp. cayenne

    In mixing bowl, combine mustard, sugar and brown sugar. Stir well until sugars are completely blended into the mustard. Add garlic powder, onion powder, smoke, paprika and cayenne. Continue mixing until well blended. Store in jar in refrigerator.

    Note: Mmm Mmm good on almost everything.

LOW COUNTRY KETCHUP

2 c. ketchup
1 tsp. garlic powder
1 tsp. onion powder
1 tsp. cayenne pepper

½ tsp. celery seed
¼ tsp. salt
2 T. beer

    In small mixing bowl, blend ketchup, garlic powder, onion powder, cayenne pepper, celery seed, salt and beer. Stir well until completely blended. Store in bottle in refrigerator.

    Note: Next time you have a cookout, this condiment is terrific on burgers, franks or sausages. Great for crispy fries and onion rings too!

Recipe Favorites

INDEX OF RECIPES

BREAKFAST, BRUNCH AND LUNCH

BEAUFORT BREAKFAST SANDWICH	9
CORN FRIED TOMATOES WITH PIMIENTO CHEESE SAUCE	10
CORNY CHICKEN SQUARES	5
CREAMED HAM OVER ONION CHEESE BISCUITS	4
DAD'S SUNDAY MORNIN' EGGS	9
DEEP SOUTH HAM AND APPLE QUICHE	12
FARM-STYLE APPLE WALNUT FRENCH TOAST	1
HARVEST-TIME GOLDEN CORN QUICHE	11
LADIES' LUNCHEON PIMIENTO CHEESE PIE	13
LOW COUNTRY CHICKEN LIVERS	12
LOW COUNTRY SPOON BREAD	14
MOLLY'S MAC 'N CHICKEN CASSEROLE	6
QUICK 'N EASY HAM 'N BISCUIT BAKE	3
RICE PLANTERS BRUNCH	13
RIVER STREET BEER BATTERED FRENCH TOAST WITH CHEESE SAUCE	2
SAVORY CRAB CHEESECAKE	14
SEASIDE MAC 'N CHEESE	8
SOUTHERN HAM 'N BISCUITS WITH COUNTRY PEPPER GRAVY	3
SPICY FISH POCKETS	8
SPICY SAVORY FRENCH TOAST WITH CHEESY CRAB SAUCE	2
SPRING GARDEN QUICHE	11
SUNRISE BREAKFAST CASSEROLE	5
THIN CRISP LEMON PANCAKES WITH SALMON DILL CHEESE	7

APPETIZERS AND SANDWICHES

APPLE CHEESEBALL	17
AUTUMN APPLE-BACON SANDWICHES	23
BOURBON GLAZED GEORGIA PECANS	15
BOURBON PEACH GLAZED LIL' SMOKIES	25
CELERY PEANUT FINGER SANDWICHES	23
CITY MARKET OLIVE SPREAD	21
CRISPY CORN PUPPIES	26
DAD'S SATURDAY AFTERNOON SANDWICHES	22
DEEP SOUTH PULLED PORK BAR-B-QUE DIP	19
GEORGIA CHEESE BALL	17
GEORGIA PEACHES 'N CREAM SPREAD	20
KEY LIME CHEESEBALL	17
LEMON TUNA SPREAD	21
LIVER 'N CHEESE PÂTÉ	18
LIVERWURST CHEESEBALL	16
MUSHROOM PUFFS	27
NUTTY PICKLE RELISH SPREAD	20
OLIVE CHEESE DELIGHTS	15
PARTY PO' BOY	25
PATIO PARTY KABOBS WITH DIPPING SAUCE	25
PECAN PRALINE CHEESE WHIP	19
PEPPER OLIVE TOASTED CHEESE SANDWICH	24
PLANTATION CHEESEBALL	16
PUMPKIN CHEESE SPREAD	21
RIVER STREET STUFFED SANDWICH WITH CREAMY ALE DRESSING	24
"SHRIMP BOAT" FINGER SANDWICHES	22
SHRIMP PUPPIES	26
SOUTHERN BLACK-EYED PEA LAYER DIP	19
SOUTHERN PEANUT AND BACON SPREAD	20
SPICY SHRIMP DIP	18
STRAWBERRY BLUSH CHEESEBALL	16
TAILGATE PASTRAMI BEER DIP	18

SOUPS AND SALADS

BLEU CHEESE AND WALNUT STUFFED PEAR SALAD	46

CHEDDAR PASTA WALDORF SALAD	38
CHICKEN PECAN SALAD	39
CHILLED PEAR SOUP	29
CITRUS CHICKEN SALAD	40
COUNTRY HARVEST APPLE SALAD	48
COUNTRY-STYLE BEET SALAD	49
CREAM OF BROCCOLI SOUP	32
CREAMY TURNIP SOUP WITH CRISPY BACON BITS	31
CRISP ICEBERG WEDGES WITH CREAMY SLAW DRESSING	50
CRISPY CHICKEN SALAD	40
DEEP SOUTH CREAM OF LIMA BEAN SOUP	33
EASY PIMIENTO CHEESE SOUP	32
GEORGIA PEACH SALAD	46
GEORGIA PEANUT SOUP	29
HAM SALAD STUFFED TOMATOES	44
HOUSEBOAT TURNIP SALAD	39
JEWELED RICE SALAD	51
LEMON SLAW	50
LOW COUNTRY CIOPPINO	37
LOW COUNTRY CREAMY SLAW	49
LOW COUNTRY POTATO SALAD	42
MAMA'S SHRIMP BISQUE	35
MARSHLAND CHICKEN AND WILD RICE SOUP	30
MELON COCKTAIL SALAD	44
MRS. RABBIT'S WINTER CARROT STEW	38
ORCHARD FRESH PEACH SOUP	30
PLANTATION CREAMY BLACK-EYED PEA SOUP WITH PIMIENTO PEPPER PURÉE	34
RIVER STREET OYSTER STEW	37
RIVER'S EDGE ROASTED POTATO SALAD	43
RIVERBOAT SWEET CORN POTATO SALAD	44
ROASTED RED PEPPER POTATO SALAD	43
SAVORY CREAMED BEET AND APPLE SALAD	49
SKIDAWAY ISLAND CORN AND CRAB CHOWDER	36
SOUTHERN CREAM OF COLLARD SOUP	33
SOUTHERN SQUASH SALAD	47
SOUTHERN TURNIP SALAD	38
SPRINGTIME JELLIED CHICKEN SALAD	41
STATELINE CITRUS-SHRIMP SALAD	42
STRAWBERRY-PEACH CREAM PARFAITS	45
SUMMER MELON SALAD	45
SUMMER PEPPER SALAD	48
SUMMER SQUASH BISQUE	35
SUMMERTIME BLACKBERRY SOUP	34
SUMMERTIME CUCUMBER SOUP	30
SUMMERTIME PEACH SOUP WITH RASPBERRY CREME	31
TOMATO AND BRUSSELS SPROUT SALAD	47
TURKEY CITRUS SALAD	41
TYBEE CREAMY SEAFOOD BISQUE	36
WILMINGTON ISLAND SALMON SALAD	48

VEGETABLES AND SIDES

BAKED POTATO CASSEROLE	68
BEER BATTERED FRIED OKRA	67
CHEESE STUFFED FRIED POTATO PUFFS	64
CHEESY TURNIP CASSEROLE	55
COUNTRY BUTTERMILK BACON WHIPPED POTATOES	63
COUNTRY GREEN BEANS AND ONIONS IN PEANUT SAUCE	55
CREAMED ONIONS AND GREEN BEANS	69
CREAMED TURNIP GREENS	56
CREAMED TURNIP ROOTS AND ONIONS	56
CREAMY TOMATO GRITS	68
DAD'S FAVORITE LIMA BEAN CASSEROLE	61
DEEP SOUTH CORNMEAL FRIED SQUASH	58
DIXIE BAKED BEANS	61
"EGG SALAD" DEVILED EGGS	54
FARMER'S MAC 'N CHEESE CASSEROLE	59

FRIED GREEN TOMATOES WITH HOT CREAMY ONION SAUCE	54
GOLDEN CORN NUGGETS	62
GOLDEN EGGPLANT BAKE	58
JEWELED SWEET POTATO BAKE	66
MAGGIE'S CHICK-A-DEE POTATOES	65
NUTTY VIDALIA ONION RINGS	60
PEPPERED GREENS	67
POTATO CHEESE BAKE	69
RIVERBOAT PUPPIES	60
SAPELO TOMATO GRITS	66
SOUTHERN CARROT FLUFF	57
SOUTHERN FRIED SQUASH PATTIES	59
SOUTHERN HOSPITALITY SUCCOTASH	57
SUNDAY AFTERNOON DEVILED EGGS	53
SWEET POTATO TURNOVERS	63
SWEET POTATO-MARSHMALLOW CRUNCH	62
TWICE BAKED SWEET POTATO BOATS	64
TYBEE ISLAND STUFFED POTATOES	66
UNCLE ROY'S FRIED POTATOES	65
ZESTY DEVILED EGGS	53

MAIN DISHES

APPLE CHEESE PORK CUTLETS	84
BLACKBERRY GLAZED CHICKEN BREASTS	74
BRANDIED PORK LOIN CHOPS WITH APPLES AND ONIONS	83
CAPE FEAR OYSTER PIES	82
CHEESY SHRIMP 'N GRITS	77
CORNBREAD STUFFED CATFISH	81
COUNTRY CHICKEN BAKE	74
DEEP SOUTH BOURBON GLAZED BURGERS	88
EASY SOUTHERN FRIED CHICKEN 'N PUFFS	72
FRIED SALMON FINGERS	81
GEORGIA PEACH GLAZED PORK RIBS AND ONIONS	85
GEORGIA SUPER DAWGS	89
GOLDEN TENDER FRIED SHRIMP	78
"HOT" FRIED CHICKEN	72
HOT 'N CRISPY FISH FILLETS	80
LOW COUNTRY PIZZA	90
LOW COUNTRY SEAFOOD LASAGNA	83
LOW COUNTRY STUFFED PEPPERS	75
LOW COUNTRY SURF 'N TURF BURGERS	88
MOON RIVER FRIED FISH FILLETS	79
MUSTARD CRUSTED PEPPER COATED HAM STEAKS	87
NUT CRUSTED DEEP FRIED CATFISH	79
PAPA'S SALISBURY STEAK SUPREME	87
RED PEPPER STUFFED CHICKEN	75
RIVER ROAD FRIED FISH FILLETS	80
RIVER ROAD HAM CAKES	86
SAUSAGE APPLE BAKE	86
SAVANNAH STYLE STUFFED CHICKEN BREASTS	77
SHRIMP CREOLE STUFFED CORNISH HENS	76
SOUTHERN COLLARD ROLLS	85
SPICY BUTTERMILK CHICKEN LIVERS WITH CREAMY GRAVY	73
SUMMERTIME LEMON FRIED CHICKEN	71
SUNDAY NIGHT CHICKEN 'N RICE CASSEROLE	73
TYBEE ISLAND BAKED EGGS AND OYSTERS	82
UNCLE NICK'S STUFFED TROUT	78
"UPTOWN" GOURMET STUFFED BURGERS	89

BREADS AND BISCUITS

BACON 'N ONION GOLDEN CORNBREAD	92
COUNTRY PEACH BREAD	91
PINKY'S OLD TIME "SWEET BISCUITS"	93
SOUTHERN BACON CHEDDAR BREAD	91
TOASTED PECAN AND BROWN SUGAR BISCUITS	92
TOASTED PECAN AND CHIVE BISCUITS	93

DESSERTS AND BEVERAGES

AUTUMN PUMPKIN PUFFS	104
BANANA CUSTARD PIE WITH PECAN PRALINE SAUCE	96
BANANAS FOSTER CRISPY RICE BARS	98
BLACKBERRY PATCH BARS	99
BLACKBERRY WALNUT CRUMB PIE	96
CHATTAHOOCHEE RIVER BLACKBERRY COBBLER	103
CHOCOLATE PECAN PIE WITH ORANGE CREAM	95
DONUT SHOP SHORTCAKE	100
FRIED APPLE STICKS	103
GINGER PEACHY CREAM SODAS	106
MACON CHERRY BLOSSOMS	100
PAPA'S BACON-PEACH MUNCHIES	105
PEANUT BUTTER AND JAM CHEESECAKE	102
PINKY'S ICEBOX PUDDIN'	97
QUICK BREAD PUDDING	102
RAISIN CHEESE PASTRY	104
RASPBERRY LIME FIZZLE	105
RIVER ROAD BREAD PUDDING WITH BOURBON SAUCE	98
SALTED PEANUT-CARAMEL ICE CREAM PIE	97
SOUTHERN "PEANUT LOG" CRISPIE BARS	99
SOUTHERN PRALINE CREAM CAKE	101
SOUTHERN SWEET CITRUS TEA	106
SPARKLING PINK LEMONADE	105
SUMMER PEACH CHEESECAKE WITH GINGER CRUST	101

RELISHES, BUTTERS AND SAUCES

BLACKBERRY BUTTER	109
BLACKBERRY RELISH	108
CORN-ON-THE-COB BUTTER	110
COUNTRY CORN RELISH	108
CREOLE MAYONNAISE	111
CREOLE TARTAR SAUCE	112
GAME TIME HOT DOG AND BURGER RELISH	109
GEORGIA PEACH BUTTER	110
HOSPITALITY BAR-B-QUE SAUCE	113
HOT 'N SPICY GARLIC BUTTER	110
LEMON TARTAR SAUCE	112
LEMON-CHEESE MAYONNAISE	111
LOW COUNTRY KETCHUP	113
OKRA AND TOMATO RELISH	107
PIMIENTO CHEESE BUTTER	109
PINEAPPLE RELISH	108
QUICK 'N EASY OLDE SOUTH BAR-B-QUE SAUCE	112
SAVORY VIDALIA PEACH RELISH	107
SOUTHERN PIMIENTO CHEESE SALAD DRESSING	111
SWEET 'N SMOKY MUSTARD	113

Ordering Cookbooks

Cookbooks make great gifts!

To order additional copies of this cookbook, contact us at:

windsongpublishing@yahoo.com

PANTRY BASICS

A WELL-STOCKED PANTRY provides all the makings for a good meal. With the right ingredients, you can quickly create a variety of satisfying, delicious meals for family or guests. Keeping these items in stock also means avoiding extra trips to the grocery store, saving you time and money. Although everyone's pantry is different, there are basic items you should always have. Add other items according to your family's needs. For example, while some families consider chips, cereals and snacks as must-haves, others can't be without feta cheese and imported olives. Use these basic pantry suggestions as a handy reference list when creating your grocery list. Don't forget refrigerated items like milk, eggs, cheese and butter.

STAPLES

- Baker's chocolate
- Baking powder
- Baking soda
- Barbeque sauce
- Bread crumbs (plain or seasoned)
- Chocolate chips
- Cocoa powder
- Cornmeal
- Cornstarch
- Crackers
- Flour
- Honey
- Ketchup
- Lemon juice
- Mayonnaise or salad dressing
- Non-stick cooking spray
- Nuts (almonds, pecans, walnuts)
- Oatmeal
- Oil (olive, vegetable)
- Pancake baking mix
- Pancake syrup
- Peanut butter
- Shortening
- Sugar (granulated, brown, powdered)
- Vinegar

PACKAGED/CANNED FOODS

- Beans (canned, dry)
- Broth (beef, chicken)
- Cake mixes with frosting
- Canned diced tomatoes
- Canned fruit
- Canned mushrooms
- Canned soup
- Canned tomato paste & sauce
- Canned tuna & chicken
- Cereal
- Dried soup mix
- Gelatin (flavored or plain)
- Gravies
- Jarred Salsa
- Milk (evaporated, sweetened condensed)
- Non-fat dry milk
- Pastas
- Rice (brown, white)
- Spaghetti sauce

SPICES/SEASONINGS

- Basil
- Bay leaves
- Black pepper
- Bouillon cubes (beef, chicken)
- Chives
- Chili powder
- Cinnamon
- Mustard (dried, prepared)
- Garlic powder or salt
- Ginger
- Nutmeg
- Onion powder or salt
- Oregano
- Paprika
- Parsley
- Rosemary
- Sage
- Salt
- Soy sauce
- Tarragon
- Thyme
- Vanilla
- Worcestershire sauce
- Yeast

Copyright © 2006
Morris Press Cookbooks
All Rights Reserved.

HERBS & SPICES

DRIED VS. FRESH. While dried herbs are convenient, they don't generally have the same purity of flavor as fresh herbs. Ensure dried herbs are still fresh by checking if they are green and not faded. Crush a few leaves to see if the aroma is still strong. Always store them in an air-tight container away from light and heat.

BASIL — Sweet, warm flavor with an aromatic odor. Use whole or ground. Good with lamb, fish, roast, stews, beef, vegetables, dressing and omelets.

BAY LEAVES — Pungent flavor. Use whole leaf but remove before serving. Good in vegetable dishes, seafood, stews and pickles.

CARAWAY — Spicy taste and aromatic smell. Use in cakes, breads, soups, cheese and sauerkraut.

CELERY SEED — Strong taste which resembles the vegetable. Can be used sparingly in pickles and chutney, meat and fish dishes, salads, bread, marinades, dressings and dips.

CHIVES — Sweet, mild flavor like that of onion. Excellent in salads, fish, soups and potatoes.

CILANTRO — Use fresh. Excellent in salads, fish, chicken, rice, beans and Mexican dishes.

CINNAMON — Sweet, pungent flavor. Widely used in many sweet baked goods, chocolate dishes, cheesecakes, pickles, chutneys and hot drinks.

CORIANDER — Mild, sweet, orangy flavor and available whole or ground. Common in curry powders and pickling spice and also used in chutney, meat dishes, casseroles, Greek-style dishes, apple pies and baked goods.

CURRY POWDER — Spices are combined to proper proportions to give a distinct flavor to meat, poultry, fish and vegetables.

DILL — Both seeds and leaves are flavorful. Leaves may be used as a garnish or cooked with fish, soup, dressings, potatoes and beans. Leaves or the whole plant may be used to flavor pickles.

FENNEL — Sweet, hot flavor. Both seeds and leaves are used. Use in small quantities in pies and baked goods. Leaves can be boiled with fish.

HERBS & SPICES

GINGER — A pungent root, this aromatic spice is sold fresh, dried or ground. Use in pickles, preserves, cakes, cookies, soups and meat dishes.

MARJORAM — May be used both dried or green. Use to flavor fish, poultry, omelets, lamb, stew, stuffing and tomato juice.

MINT — Aromatic with a cool flavor. Excellent in beverages, fish, lamb, cheese, soup, peas, carrots and fruit desserts.

NUTMEG — Whole or ground. Used in chicken and cream soups, cheese dishes, fish cakes, and with chicken and veal. Excellent in custards, milk puddings, pies and cakes.

OREGANO — Strong, aromatic odor. Use whole or ground in tomato juice, fish, eggs, pizza, omelets, chili, stew, gravy, poultry and vegetables.

PAPRIKA — A bright red pepper, this spice is used in meat, vegetables and soups or as a garnish for potatoes, salads or eggs.

PARSLEY — Best when used fresh, but can be used dried as a garnish or as a seasoning. Try in fish, omelets, soup, meat, stuffing and mixed greens.

ROSEMARY — Very aromatic. Can be used fresh or dried. Season fish, stuffing, beef, lamb, poultry, onions, eggs, bread and potatoes. Great in dressings.

SAFFRON — Aromatic, slightly bitter taste. Only a pinch needed to flavor and color dishes such as bouillabaisse, chicken soup, rice, paella, fish sauces, buns and cakes. Very expensive, so where a touch of color is needed, use turmeric instead, but the flavor will not be the same.

SAGE — Use fresh or dried. The flowers are sometimes used in salads. May be used in tomato juice, fish, omelets, beef, poultry, stuffing, cheese spreads and breads.

TARRAGON — Leaves have a pungent, hot taste. Use to flavor sauces, salads, fish, poultry, tomatoes, eggs, green beans, carrots and dressings.

THYME — Sprinkle leaves on fish or poultry before broiling or baking. Throw a few sprigs directly on coals shortly before meat is finished grilling.

TURMERIC — Aromatic, slightly bitter flavor. Should be used sparingly in curry powder and relishes and to color cakes and rice dishes.

Use 3 times more fresh herbs if substituting fresh for dried.

BAKING BREADS

HINTS FOR BAKING BREADS

- Kneading dough for 30 seconds after mixing improves the texture of baking powder biscuits.

- Instead of shortening, use cooking or salad oil in waffles and hot cakes.

- When bread is baking, a small dish of water in the oven will help keep the crust from hardening.

- Dip a spoon in hot water to measure shortening, butter, etc., and the fat will slip out more easily.

- Small amounts of leftover corn may be added to pancake batter for variety.

- To make bread crumbs, use the fine cutter of a food grinder and tie a large paper bag over the spout in order to prevent flying crumbs.

- When you are doing any sort of baking, you get better results if you remember to preheat your cookie sheet, muffin tins or cake pans.

3 RULES FOR USE OF LEAVENING AGENTS

1. In simple flour mixtures, use 2 teaspoons baking powder to leaven 1 cup flour. Reduce this amount ½ teaspoon for each egg used.

2. To 1 teaspoon soda, use 2 ¼ teaspoons cream of tartar, 2 cups freshly soured milk or 1 cup molasses.

3. To substitute soda and an acid for baking powder, divide the amount of baking powder by 4. Take that as your measure and add acid according to rule 2.

PROPORTIONS OF BAKING POWDER TO FLOUR

biscuits	to 1 cup flour use 1 ¼ tsp. baking powder
cake with oil	to 1 cup flour use 1 tsp. baking powder
muffins	to 1 cup flour use 1 ½ tsp. baking powder
popovers	to 1 cup flour use 1 ¼ tsp. baking powder
waffles	to 1 cup flour use 1 ¼ tsp. baking powder

PROPORTIONS OF LIQUID TO FLOUR

pour batter	to 1 cup liquid use 1 cup flour
drop batter	to 1 cup liquid use 2 to 2 ½ cups flour
soft dough	to 1 cup liquid use 3 to 3 ½ cups flour
stiff dough	to 1 cup liquid use 4 cups flour

TIME & TEMPERATURE CHART

Breads	Minutes	Temperature
biscuits	12 - 15	400° - 450°
cornbread	25 - 30	400° - 425°
gingerbread	40 - 50	350° - 370°
loaf	50 - 60	350° - 400°
nut bread	50 - 75	350°
popovers	30 - 40	425° - 450°
rolls	20 - 30	400° - 450°

BAKING DESSERTS

PERFECT COOKIES

Cookie dough that must be rolled is much easier to handle after it has been refrigerated for 10 to 30 minutes. This keeps the dough from sticking, even though it may be soft. If not done, the soft dough may require more flour and too much flour makes cookies hard and brittle. Place on a floured board only as much dough as can be easily managed. Flour the rolling pin slightly and roll lightly to desired thickness. Cut shapes close together and add trimmings to dough that needs to be rolled. Place pans or sheets in upper third of oven. Watch cookies carefully while baking in order to avoid burned edges. When sprinkling sugar on cookies, try putting it into a salt shaker in order to save time.

PERFECT PIES

- Pie crust will be better and easier to make if all the ingredients are cool.

- The lower crust should be placed in the pan so that it covers the surface smoothly. Air pockets beneath the surface will push the crust out of shape while baking.

- Folding the top crust over the lower crust before crimping will keep juices in the pie.

- When making custard pie, bake at a high temperature for about 10 minutes to prevent a soggy crust. Then finish baking at a low temperature.

- When making cream pie, sprinkle crust with powdered sugar in order to prevent it from becoming soggy.

PERFECT CAKES

- Fill cake pans two-thirds full and spread batter into corners and sides, leaving a slight hollow in the center.

- Cake is done when it shrinks from the sides of the pan or if it springs back when touched lightly with the finger.

- After removing a cake from the oven, place it on a rack for about 5 minutes. Then, the sides should be loosened and the cake turned out on a rack in order to finish cooling.

- Do not frost cakes until thoroughly cool.

- Icing will remain where you put it if you sprinkle cake with powdered sugar first.

TIME & TEMPERATURE CHART

Dessert	Time	Temperature
butter cake, layer	20 - 40 min.	380° - 400°
butter cake, loaf	40 - 60 min.	360° - 400°
cake, angel	50 - 60 min.	300° - 360°
cake, fruit	3 - 4 hrs.	275° - 325°
cake, sponge	40 - 60 min.	300° - 350°
cookies, molasses	18 - 20 min.	350° - 375°
cookies, thin	10 - 12 min.	380° - 390°
cream puffs	45 - 60 min.	300° - 350°
meringue	40 - 60 min.	250° - 300°
pie crust	20 - 40 min.	400° - 500°

VEGETABLES & FRUITS

COOKING TIME TABLE

Vegetable	Cooking Method	Time
artichokes	boiled	40 min.
	steamed	45 - 60 min.
asparagus tips	boiled	10 - 15 min.
beans, lima	boiled	20 - 40 min.
	steamed	60 min.
beans, string	boiled	15 - 35 min.
	steamed	60 min.
beets, old	boiled or steamed	1 - 2 hours.
beets, young with skin	boiled	30 min.
	steamed	60 min.
	baked	70 - 90 min.
broccoli, flowerets	boiled	5 - 10 min.
broccoli, stems	boiled	20 - 30 min.
brussels sprouts	boiled	20 - 30 min.
cabbage, chopped	boiled	10 - 20 min.
	steamed	25 min.
carrots, cut across	boiled	8 - 10 min.
	steamed	40 min.
cauliflower, flowerets	boiled	8 - 10 min.
cauliflower, stem down	boiled	20 - 30 min.
corn, green, tender	boiled	5 - 10 min.
	steamed	15 min.
	baked	20 min.
corn on the cob	boiled	8 - 10 min.
	steamed	15 min.
eggplant, whole	boiled	30 min.
	steamed	40 min.
	baked	45 min.
parsnips	boiled	25 - 40 min.
	steamed	60 min.
	baked	60 - 75 min.
peas, green	boiled or steamed	5 - 15 min.
potatoes	boiled	20 - 40 min.
	steamed	60 min.
	baked	45 - 60 min.
pumpkin or squash	boiled	20 - 40 min.
	steamed	45 min.
	baked	60 min.
tomatoes	boiled	5 - 15 min.
turnips	boiled	25 - 40 min.

DRYING TIME TABLE

Fruit	Sugar or Honey	Cooking Time
apricots	¼ c. for each cup of fruit	about 40 min.
figs	1 T. for each cup of fruit	about 30 min.
peaches	¼ c. for each cup of fruit	about 45 min.
prunes	2 T. for each cup of fruit	about 45 min.

VEGETABLES & FRUITS

BUYING FRESH VEGETABLES

Artichokes: Look for compact, tightly closed heads with green, clean-looking leaves. Avoid those with leaves that are brown or separated.

Asparagus: Stalks should be tender and firm; tips should be close and compact. Choose the stalks with very little white; they are more tender. Use asparagus soon because it toughens quickly.

Beans, Snap: Those with small seeds inside the pods are best. Avoid beans with dry-looking pods.

Broccoli, Brussels Sprouts and Cauliflower: Flower clusters on broccoli and cauliflower should be tight and close together. Brussels sprouts should be firm and compact. Smudgy, dirty spots may indicate pests or disease.

Cabbage and Head Lettuce: Choose heads that are heavy for their size. Avoid cabbage with worm holes and lettuce with discoloration or soft rot.

Cucumbers: Choose long, slender cucumbers for best quality. May be dark or medium green, but yellow ones are undesirable.

Mushrooms: Caps should be closed around the stems. Avoid black or brown gills.

Peas and Lima Beans: Select pods that are well-filled but not bulging. Avoid dried, spotted, yellow or limp pods.

BUYING FRESH FRUITS

Bananas: Skin should be free of bruises and black or brown spots. Purchase them slightly green and allow them to ripen at room temperature.

Berries: Select plump, solid berries with good color. Avoid stained containers which indicate wet or leaky berries. Berries with clinging caps, such as blackberries and raspberries, may be unripe. Strawberries without caps may be overripe.

Melons: In cantaloupes, thick, close netting on the rind indicates best quality. Cantaloupes are ripe when the stem scar is smooth and the space between the netting is yellow or yellow-green. They are best when fully ripe with fruity odor.

Honeydews are ripe when rind has creamy to yellowish color and velvety texture. Immature honeydews are whitish-green.

Ripe watermelons have some yellow color on one side. If melons are white or pale green on one side, they are not ripe.

Oranges, Grapefruit and Lemons: Choose those heavy for their size. Smoother, thinner skins usually indicate more juice. Most skin markings do not affect quality. Oranges with a slight greenish tinge may be just as ripe as fully colored ones. Light or greenish-yellow lemons are more tart than deep yellow ones. Avoid citrus fruits showing withered, sunken or soft areas.

NAPKIN FOLDING

FOR BEST RESULTS, use well-starched linen napkins if possible. For more complicated folds, 24-inch napkins work best. Practice the folds with newspapers. Children will have fun decorating the table once they learn these attractive folds!

SHIELD

Easy fold. Elegant with monogram in corner.

Instructions:
1. Fold into quarter size. If monogrammed, ornate corner should face down.
2. Turn up folded corner three-quarters.
3. Overlap right side and left side points.
4. Turn over; adjust sides so they are even, single point in center.
5. Place point up or down on plate, or left of plate.

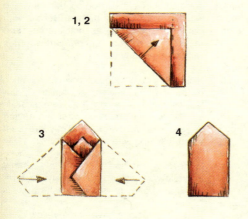

ROSETTE

Elegant on plate.

Instructions:
1. Fold left and right edges to center, leaving 1/2" opening along center.
2. Pleat firmly from top edge to bottom edge. Sharpen edges with hot iron.
3. Pinch center together. If necessary, use small piece of pipe cleaner to secure and top with single flower.
4. Spread out rosette.

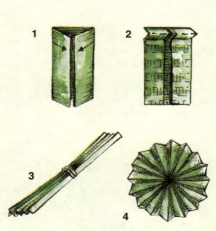

NAPKIN FOLDING

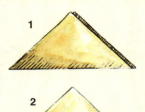

CANDLE

Easy to do; can be decorated.

Instructions:
1. Fold into triangle, point at top.
2. Turn lower edge up 1".
3. Turn over, folded edge down.
4. Roll tightly from left to right.
5. Tuck in corner. Stand upright.

FAN

Pretty in napkin ring or on plate.

Instructions:
1. Fold top and bottom edges to center.
2. Fold top and bottom edges to center a second time.
3. Pleat firmly from the left edge. Sharpen edges with hot iron.
4. Spread out fan. Balance flat folds of each side on table. Well-starched napkins will hold shape.

LILY

Effective and pretty on table.

Instructions:
1. Fold napkin into quarters.
2. Fold into triangle, closed corner to open points.
3. Turn two points over to other side. (Two points are on either side of closed point.)
4. Pleat.
5. Place closed end in glass. Pull down two points on each side and shape.

MEASUREMENTS & SUBSTITUTIONS

MEASUREMENTS

a pinch	1/8 teaspoon or less
3 teaspoons	1 tablespoon
4 tablespoons	1/4 cup
8 tablespoons	1/2 cup
12 tablespoons	3/4 cup
16 tablespoons	1 cup
2 cups	1 pint
4 cups	1 quart
4 quarts	1 gallon
8 quarts	1 peck
4 pecks	1 bushel
16 ounces	1 pound
32 ounces	1 quart
1 ounce liquid	2 tablespoons
8 ounces liquid	1 cup

Use standard measuring spoons and cups. All measurements are level.

C° TO F° CONVERSION

120° C	250° F
140° C	275° F
150° C	300° F
160° C	325° F
180° C	350° F
190° C	375° F
200° C	400° F
220° C	425° F
230° C	450° F

Temperature conversions are estimates.

SUBSTITUTIONS

Ingredient	Quantity	Substitute
baking powder	1 teaspoon	1/4 tsp. baking soda plus 1/2 tsp. cream of tartar
chocolate	1 square (1 oz.)	3 or 4 T. cocoa plus 1 T. butter
cornstarch	1 tablespoon	2 T. flour or 2 tsp. quick-cooking tapioca
cracker crumbs	3/4 cup	1 c. bread crumbs
dates	1 lb.	1 1/2 c. dates, pitted and cut
dry mustard	1 teaspoon	1 T. prepared mustard
flour, self-rising	1 cup	1 c. all-purpose flour, 1/2 tsp. salt, and 1 tsp. baking powder
herbs, fresh	1 tablespoon	1 tsp. dried herbs
ketchup or chili sauce	1 cup	1 c. tomato sauce plus 1/2 c. sugar and 2 T. vinegar (for use in cooking)
milk, sour	1 cup	1 T. lemon juice or vinegar plus sweet milk to make 1 c. (let stand 5 minutes)
whole	1 cup	1/2 c. evaporated milk plus 1/2 c. water
min. marshmallows	10	1 lg. marshmallow
onion, fresh	1 small	1 T. instant minced onion, rehydrated
sugar, brown	1/2 cup	2 T. molasses in 1/2 c. granulated sugar
powdered	1 cup	1 c. granulated sugar plus 1 tsp. cornstarch
tomato juice	1 cup	1/2 c. tomato sauce plus 1/2 c. water

When substituting cocoa for chocolate in cakes, the amount of flour must be reduced. Brown and white sugars usually can be interchanged.

EQUIVALENCY CHART

Food	Quantity	Yield
apple	1 medium	1 cup
banana, mashed	1 medium	1/3 cup
bread	1 1/2 slices	1 cup soft crumbs
bread	1 slice	1/4 cup fine, dry crumbs
butter	1 stick or 1/4 pound	1/2 cup
cheese, American, cubed	1 pound	2 2/3 cups
American, grated	1 pound	5 cups
cream cheese	3-ounce package	6 2/3 tablespoons
chocolate, bitter	1 square	1 ounce
cocoa	1 pound	4 cups
coconut	1 1/2 pound package	2 2/3 cups
coffee, ground	1 pound	5 cups
cornmeal	1 pound	3 cups
cornstarch	1 pound	3 cups
crackers, graham	14 squares	1 cup fine crumbs
saltine	28 crackers	1 cup fine crumbs
egg	4 - 5 whole	1 cup
whites	8 - 10	1 cup
yolks	10 - 12	1 cup
evaporated milk	1 cup	3 cups whipped
flour, cake, sifted	1 pound	4 1/2 cups
rye	1 pound	5 cups
white, sifted	1 pound	4 cups
white, unsifted	1 pound	3 3/4 cups
gelatin, flavored	3 1/4 ounces	1/2 cup
unflavored	1/4 ounce	1 tablespoon
lemon	1 medium	3 tablespoon juice
marshmallows	16	1/4 pound
noodles, cooked	8-ounce package	7 cups
uncooked	4 ounces (1 1/2 cups)	2 - 3 cups cooked
macaroni, cooked	8-ounce package	6 cups
macaroni, uncooked	4 ounces (1 1/4 cups)	2 1/4 cups cooked
spaghetti, uncooked	7 ounces	4 cups cooked
nuts, chopped	1/4 pound	1 cup
almonds	1 pound	3 1/2 cups
walnuts, broken	1 pound	3 cups
walnuts, unshelled	1 pound	1 1/2 to 1 3/4 cups
onion	1 medium	1/2 cup
orange	3 - 4 medium	1 cup juice
raisins	1 pound	3 1/2 cups
rice, brown	1 cup	4 cups cooked
converted	1 cup	3 1/2 cups cooked
regular	1 cup	3 cups cooked
wild	1 cup	4 cups cooked
sugar, brown	1 pound	2 1/2 cups
powdered	1 pound	3 1/2 cups
white	1 pound	2 cups
vanilla wafers	22	1 cup fine crumbs
zwieback, crumbled	4	1 cup

FOOD QUANTITIES

FOR LARGE SERVINGS

	25 Servings	50 Servings	100 Servings
Beverages:			
coffee	1/2 pound & 1 1/2 gallons water	1 pound & 3 gallons water	2 pounds & 6 gallons water
lemonade	10-15 lemons & 1 1/2 gallons water	20-30 lemons & 3 gallons water	40-60 lemons & 6 gallons water
tea	1/12 pound & 1 1/2 gallons water	1/6 pound & 3 gallons water	1/3 pound & 6 gallons water
Desserts:			
layered cake	1 12" cake	3 10" cakes	6 10" cakes
sheet cake	1 10" x 12" cake	1 12" x 20" cake	2 12" x 20" cakes
watermelon	37 1/2 pounds	75 pounds	150 pounds
whipping cream	3/4 pint	1 1/2 to 2 pints	3-4 pints
Ice cream:			
brick	3 1/4 quarts	6 1/2 quarts	13 quarts
bulk	2 1/4 quarts	4 1/2 quarts or 1 1/4 gallons	9 quarts or 2 1/2 gallons
Meat, poultry or fish:			
fish	13 pounds	25 pounds	50 pounds
fish, fillets or steak	7 1/2 pounds	15 pounds	30 pounds
hamburger	9 pounds	18 pounds	35 pounds
turkey or chicken	13 pounds	25-35 pounds	50-75 pounds
wieners (beef)	6 1/2 pounds	13 pounds	25 pounds
Salads, casseroles:			
baked beans	3/4 gallon	1 1/4 gallons	2 1/2 gallons
jello salad	3/4 gallon	1 1/4 gallons	2 1/2 gallons
potato salad	4 1/4 quarts	2 1/4 gallons	4 1/2 gallons
scalloped potatoes	4 1/2 quarts or 1 12" x 20" pan	9 quarts or 2 1/4 gallons	18 quarts 4 1/2 gallons
spaghetti	1 1/4 gallons	2 1/2 gallons	5 gallons
Sandwiches:			
bread	50 slices or 3 1-lb. loaves	100 slices or 6 1-lb. loaves	200 slices or 12 1-lb. loaves
butter	1/2 pound	1 pound	2 pounds
lettuce	1 1/2 heads	3 heads	6 heads
mayonnaise	1 cup	2 cups	4 cups
mixed filling			
meat, eggs, fish	1 1/2 quarts	3 quarts	6 quarts
jam, jelly	1 quart	2 quarts	4 quarts

QUICK FIXES

PRACTICALLY EVERYONE has experienced that dreadful moment in the kitchen when a recipe failed and dinner guests have arrived. Perhaps a failed timer, distraction or a missing or mismeasured ingredient is to blame. These handy tips can save the day!

Acidic foods – Sometimes a tomato-based sauce will become too acidic. Add baking soda, one teaspoon at a time, to the sauce. Use sugar as a sweeter alternative.

Burnt food on pots and pans – Allow the pan to cool on its own. Remove as much of the food as possible. Fill with hot water and add a capful of liquid fabric softener to the pot; let it stand for a few hours. You'll have an easier time removing the burnt food.

Chocolate seizes – Chocolate can seize (turn coarse and grainy) when it comes into contact with water. Place seized chocolate in a metal bowl over a large saucepan with an inch of simmering water in it. Over medium heat, slowly whisk in warm heavy cream. Use 1/4 cup cream to 4 ounces of chocolate. The chocolate will melt and become smooth.

Forgot to thaw whipped topping – Thaw in microwave for 1 minute on the defrost setting. Stir to blend well. Do not over thaw!

Hands smell like garlic or onion – Rinse hands under cold water while rubbing them with a large stainless steel spoon.

Hard brown sugar – Place in a paper bag and microwave for a few seconds, or place hard chunks in a food processor.

Jell-O too hard – Heat on a low microwave power setting for a very short time.

Lumpy gravy or sauce – Use a blender, food processor or simply strain.

No tomato juice – Mix 1/2 cup ketchup with 1/2 cup water.

Out of honey – Substitute 1 1/4 cups sugar dissolved in 1 cup water.

Overcooked sweet potatoes or carrots – Softened sweet potatoes and carrots make a wonderful soufflé with the addition of eggs and sugar. Consult your favorite cookbook for a good soufflé recipe. Overcooked sweet potatoes can also be used as pie filling.

Sandwich bread is stale – Toast or microwave bread briefly. Otherwise, turn it into bread crumbs. Bread exposed to light and heat will hasten its demise, so consider using a bread box. If the bread will not be eaten within a few days, store half in the freezer.

Soup, sauce, gravy too thin – Add 1 tablespoon of flour to hot soup, sauce or gravy. Whisk well (to avoid lumps) while the mixture is boiling. Repeat if necessary.

Sticky rice – Rinse rice with warm water.

Stew or soup is greasy – Refrigerate and remove grease once it congeals. Another trick is to lay cold lettuce leaves over the hot stew for about 10 seconds and then remove. Repeat as necessary.

Too salty – Add a little sugar and vinegar. For soups or sauces, add a raw peeled potato.

Too sweet – Add a little vinegar or lemon juice.

Undercooked cakes and cookies – Serve over vanilla ice cream. You can also layer pieces of cake or cookies with whipped cream and fresh fruit to form a dessert parfait. Crumbled cookies also make an excellent ice cream or cream pie topping.

COUNTING CALORIES

BEVERAGES

apple juice, 6 oz.	90
coffee (black)	0
cola, 12 oz.	115
cranberry juice, 6 oz.	115
ginger ale, 12 oz.	115
grape juice, (prepared from frozen concentrate), 6 oz.	142
lemonade, (prepared from frozen concentrate), 6 oz.	85
milk, protein fortified, 1 c.	105
skim, 1 c.	90
whole, 1 c.	160
orange juice, 6 oz.	85
pineapple juice, unsweetened, 6 oz.	95
root beer, 12 oz.	150
tonic (quinine water) 12 oz.	132

BREADS

cornbread, 1 sm. square	130
dumplings, 1 med.	70
French toast, 1 slice	135
melba toast, 1 slice	25
muffins, blueberry, 1 muffin	110
bran, 1 muffin	106
corn, 1 muffin	125
English, 1 muffin	280
pancakes, 1 (4-in.)	60
pumpernickel, 1 slice	75
rye, 1 slice	60
waffle, 1	216
white, 1 slice	60 - 70
whole wheat, 1 slice	55 - 65

CEREALS

cornflakes, 1 c.	105
cream of wheat, 1 c.	120
oatmeal, 1 c.	148
rice flakes, 1 c.	105
shredded wheat, 1 biscuit	100
sugar krisps, 3/4 c.	110

CRACKERS

graham, 1 cracker	15 - 30
rye crisp, 1 cracker	35
saltine, 1 cracker	17 - 20
wheat thins, 1 cracker	9

DAIRY PRODUCTS

butter or margarine, 1 T.	100
cheese, American, 1 oz.	100
camembert, 1 oz.	85
cheddar, 1 oz.	115
cottage cheese, 1 oz.	30
mozzarella, 1 oz.	90
parmesan, 1 oz.	130
ricotta, 1 oz.	50
roquefort, 1 oz.	105
Swiss, 1 oz.	105
cream, light, 1 T.	30
heavy, 1 T.	55
sour, 1 T.	45
hot chocolate, with milk, 1 c.	277
milk chocolate, 1 oz.	145 - 155
yogurt made w/ whole milk, 1 c.	150 - 165
made w/ skimmed milk, 1 c.	125

EGGS

fried, 1 lg.	100
poached or boiled, 1 lg.	75 - 80
scrambled or in omelet, 1 lg.	110 - 130

FISH & SEAFOOD

bass, 4 oz.	105
salmon, broiled or baked, 3 oz.	155
sardines, canned in oil, 3 oz.	170
trout, fried, 3 1/2 oz.	220
tuna, in oil, 3 oz.	170
in water, 3 oz.	110

COUNTING CALORIES

FRUITS

apple, 1 med.	80 - 100
applesauce, sweetened, ½ c.	90 - 115
unsweetened, ½ c.	50
banana, 1 med.	85
blueberries, ½ c.	45
cantaloupe, ½ c.	24
cherries (pitted), raw, ½ c.	40
grapefruit, ½ med.	55
grapes, ½ c.	35 - 55
honeydew, ½ c.	55
mango, 1 med.	90
orange, 1 med.	65 - 75
peach, 1 med.	35
pear, 1 med.	60 - 100
pineapple, fresh, ½ c.	40
canned in syrup, ½ c.	95
plum, 1 med.	30
strawberries, fresh, ½ c.	30
frozen and sweetened, ½ c.	120 - 140
tangerine, 1 lg.	39
watermelon, ½ c.	42

MEAT & POULTRY

beef, ground (lean), 3 oz.	185
roast, 3 oz.	185
chicken, broiled, 3 oz.	115
lamb chop (lean), 3 oz.	175 - 200
steak, sirloin, 3 oz.	175
tenderloin, 3 oz.	174
top round, 3 oz.	162
turkey, dark meat, 3 oz.	175
white meat, 3 oz.	150
veal, cutlet, 3 oz.	156
roast, 3 oz.	76

NUTS

almonds, 2 T.	105
cashews, 2 T.	100
peanuts, 2 T.	105
peanut butter, 1 T.	95
pecans, 2 T.	95
pistachios, 2 T.	92
walnuts, 2 T.	80

PASTA

macaroni or spaghetti, cooked, ¾ c.	115

SALAD DRESSINGS

blue cheese, 1 T.	70
French, 1 T.	65
Italian, 1 T.	80
mayonnaise, 1 T.	100
olive oil, 1 T.	124
Russian, 1 T.	70
salad oil, 1 T.	120

SOUPS

bean, 1 c.	130 - 180
beef noodle, 1 c.	70
bouillon and consomme, 1 c.	30
chicken noodle, 1 c.	65
chicken with rice, 1 c.	50
minestrone, 1 c.	80 - 150
split pea, 1 c.	145 - 170
tomato with milk, 1 c.	170
vegetable, 1 c.	80 - 100

VEGETABLES

asparagus, 1 c.	35
broccoli, cooked, ½ c.	25
cabbage, cooked, ½ c.	15 - 20
carrots, cooked, ½ c.	25 - 30
cauliflower, ½ c.	10 - 15
corn (kernels), ½ c.	70
green beans, 1 c.	30
lettuce, shredded, ½ c.	5
mushrooms, canned, ½ c.	20
onions, cooked, ½ c.	30
peas, cooked, ½ c.	60
potato, baked, 1 med.	90
chips, 8-10	100
mashed, w/milk & butter, 1 c.	200 - 300
spinach, 1 c.	40
tomato, raw, 1 med.	25
cooked, ½ c.	30

COOKING TERMS

Au gratin: Topped with crumbs and/or cheese and browned in oven or under broiler.

Au jus: Served in its own juices.

Baste: To moisten foods during cooking with pan drippings or special sauce in order to add flavor and prevent drying.

Bisque: A thick cream soup.

Blanch: To immerse in rapidly boiling water and allow to cook slightly.

Cream: To soften a fat, especially butter, by beating it at room temperature. Butter and sugar are often creamed together, making a smooth, soft paste.

Crimp: To seal the edges of a two-crust pie either by pinching them at intervals with the fingers or by pressing them together with the tines of a fork.

Crudités: An assortment of raw vegetables (i.e. carrots, broccoli, celery, mushrooms) that is served as an hors d'oeuvre, often accompanied by a dip.

Degrease: To remove fat from the surface of stews, soups or stock. Usually cooled in the refrigerator so that fat hardens and is easily removed.

Dredge: To coat lightly with flour, cornmeal, etc.

Entrée: The main course.

Fold: To incorporate a delicate substance, such as whipped cream or beaten egg whites, into another substance without releasing air bubbles. A spatula is used to gently bring part of the mixture from the bottom of the bowl to the top. The process is repeated, while slowly rotating the bowl, until the ingredients are thoroughly blended.

Glaze: To cover with a glossy coating, such as a melted and somewhat diluted jelly for fruit desserts.

Julienne: To cut or slice vegetables, fruits or cheeses into match-shaped slivers.

Marinate: To allow food to stand in a liquid in order to tenderize or to add flavor.

Meuniére: Dredged with flour and sautéed in butter.

Mince: To chop food into very small pieces.

Parboil: To boil until partially cooked; to blanch. Usually final cooking in a seasoned sauce follows this procedure.

Pare: To remove the outermost skin of a fruit or vegetable.

Poach: To cook gently in hot liquid kept just below the boiling point.

Purée: To mash foods by hand by rubbing through a sieve or food mill, or by whirling in a blender or food processor until perfectly smooth.

Refresh: To run cold water over food that has been parboiled in order to stop the cooking process quickly.

Sauté: To cook and/or brown food in a small quantity of hot shortening.

Scald: To heat to just below the boiling point, when tiny bubbles appear at the edge of the saucepan.

Simmer: To cook in liquid just below the boiling point. The surface of the liquid should be barely moving, broken from time to time by slowly rising bubbles.

Steep: To let food stand in hot liquid in order to extract or to enhance flavor, like tea in hot water or poached fruit in syrup.

Toss: To combine ingredients with a repeated lifting motion.

Whip: To beat rapidly in order to incorporate air and produce expansion, as in heavy cream or egg whites.